P9-DEM-850

Praise for *If You Want to Walk on Water, You've Got to Get Out of the Boat*

John Ortberg is profound without being heavy. The message is clear and absolutely basic: You get to live in God's care and power when, through confidence in Jesus, you step out of the arrangements you have made to keep yourself safe. That is how to find the kingdom of God, as everyday reality. So find your boat and step out of it. And you will know first-hand the life of faith others only talk about.

DALLAS WILLARD, AUTHOR, *THE DIVINE CONSPIRACY*

With an engaging and compelling style, John Ortberg leads the reader on a great adventure. But it's an adventure that can only happen when you say "yes" to making Jesus the focus of your life. Open the covers of this book and discover the incredible opportunities God has waiting for you.

BOB BUFORD, AUTHOR, *HALFTIME*

I read *If You Want to Walk on Water* in one sitting. I didn't want to, but I made the mistake of starting. I was laughing before I finished the first page and hooked by the middle of chapter one. John Ortberg is one of my all-time favorite authors. His humor coupled with his honest and practical approach to Christian growth is so refreshing. If you want to walk on water, read this book, THEN get out of the boat and live!

KEN DAVIS, AUTHOR AND SPEAKER

This book is pure Ortberg — insightful and profound, winsome and funny, motivating and challenging. John does through this book what he does for me as a friend: lovingly but persistently prods me to keep growing!

LEE STROBEL, AUTHOR,
THE CASE FOR CHRIST AND THE CASE FOR FAITH

Resources by John Ortberg

Everybody's Normal Till You Get to Know Them
(book, ebook, audio)

God Is Closer Than You Think
(book, ebook, audio, curriculum with Stephen and Amanda Sorenson)

*If You Want to Walk on Water,
You've Got to Get Out of the Boat*
(book, ebook, audio, curriculum with Stephen and Amanda Sorenson)

Know Doubt
(book, ebook, previously titled Faith and Doubt)

The Life You've Always Wanted
(book, ebook, audio, curriculum with Stephen and Amanda Sorenson)

Love Beyond Reason

The Me I Want to Be
(book, ebook, audio, curriculum with Scott Rubin)

Soul Keeping
(book, ebook, curriculum with Christine M. Anderson)

When the Game Is Over, It All Goes Back in the Box
(book, ebook, audio, curriculum with Stephen and Amanda Sorenson)

Who Is This Man?
(book, ebook, audio, curriculum with Christine M. Anderson)

IF YOU WANT TO
WALK ON
WATER
YOU'VE GOT TO
GET OUT OF THE
BOAT

To Sam Reeves and Max DePree,
who have taught me so much
about getting out of the boat

IF YOU WANT TO
WALK ON
WATER
YOU'VE GOT TO
GET OUT OF THE
BOAT

JOHN ORTBERG

ZONDERVAN®
.com

WILLOW
Willow Creek Resources

ZONDERVAN

If You Want to Walk on Water, You've Got to Get Out of the Boat
Copyright © 2001 by John Ortberg

This title is also available as a Zondervan ebook.
Visit www.zondervan.com/ebooks.

This title is also available in a Zondervan audio edition.
Visit www.zondervan.fm.

Requests for information should be addressed to:

Zondervan, 3900 *Sparks Dr. SE, Grand Rapids, Michigan 49546*

This edition: ISBN 978-0-310-34046-1 (softcover)

Library of Congress Cataloging-in-Publication Data

Ortberg, John.
 If you want to walk on water, you've got to get out of the boat / John Ortberg.
  p. cm.
 Includes bibliographical references.
 ISBN 978-0-310-22863-9 (hardcover)
 1. Trust in God—Christianity. 2. Bible N.T. Matthew XIV, 22–33—Criticism,
interpretation, etc. I. Title.
BV4637 .O78 2000
248.4—dc21   00-047714

All Scripture quotations, unless otherwise indicated, are taken from the *New Revised Standard
Version Bible*, copyright © 1989 by the Division of Christian Education of the National Council
of the Churches of Christ in the United States of America. Used by permission of Zondervan.
All rights reserved.

Citations in chapter 7 from Parker Palmer, *Let Your Life Speak*, copyright © 2000 by Parker
Palmer, are reprinted by permission of Jossey-Bass, Inc., a subsidary of John Wiley & Sons, Inc.

Any Internet addresses (websites, blogs, etc.) and telephone numbers in this book are offered
as a resource. They are not intended in any way to be or imply an endorsement by Zondervan,
nor does Zondervan vouch for the content of these sites and numbers for the life of this book.

All rights reserved. No part of this publication may be reproduced, stored in a retrieval system,
or transmitted in any form or by any means—electronic, mechanical, photocopy, recording, or
any other—except for brief quotations in printed reviews, without the prior permission of the
publisher.

Interior design by Melissa Elenbaas

Printed in the United States of America

Contents

And early in the morning he came walking toward them on the sea. But when the disciples saw him walking on the sea, they were terrified, saying, "It is a ghost!" And they cried out in fear. But immediately Jesus spoke to them and said, "Take heart, it is I; do not be afraid."

Peter answered him, "Lord, if it is you, command me to come to you on the water." He said, "Come." So Peter got out of the boat, started walking on the water, and came toward Jesus. But when he noticed the strong wind, he became frightened, and beginning to sink, he cried out, "Lord, save me!" Jesus immediately reached out his hand and caught him, saying to him, "You of little faith, why did you doubt?"

When they got into the boat, the wind ceased. And those in the boat worshiped him, saying, "Truly you are the Son of God."

Matthew 14:25–32

Preface

I want to invite you to go for a walk.

The Bible is, among other things, a list of unforgettable walks. The first one was taken by God himself, who, we are told, used to walk in the garden in the cool of the day. But as a general rule, God asked people to walk with him.

There was the hard walk that Abraham took with his son Isaac on the road to Moriah. There was the liberating walk Moses and the Israelites took through the path that was normally occupied by the Red Sea, and the frustrating walk that took them on the roundabout way of the desert for forty years. There was Joshua's triumphant walk around Jericho, the disciples' illuminating walk to Emmaus, Paul's interrupted walk to Damascus. There was the walk so sad and holy that it received its own name: the walk from the Praetorium to Golgotha called the *Via Dolorosa*—the way of great sorrow.

But perhaps the most unforgettable walk of all was taken by Peter the day he got out of a boat and walked on the water. It is unforgettable not so much because of where he was walking as what he was walking *on* and who he was walking *with*. I think that when Peter went treading on the waves he was experiencing walking at its finest.

In this book, let Peter's walk stand as an invitation to everyone who, like him, wants to step out in faith, who wants to experience something more of the power and presence of God. Let water-walking be a picture of doing with God's help what I could never do on my own. How does such a thing come about? There is a consistent pattern in Scripture of what happens in a life that God wants to use and improve:

—There is always a call. God asks an ordinary person to engage in an act of extraordinary trust, that of getting out of the boat.

—There is always fear. God has an inextinguishable habit of asking people to do things that are scary to them. It may be a fear of inadequacy ("I am slow of speech and slow of tongue," Moses said.) It may be a fear of failure ("The land we explored devours those who live in it," cried the spies sent out to the Promised Land). It may even be a fear of God ("For I knew you were a hard man, seeking to reap where you did not sow," claimed the servant in Jesus' parable). But one way or another, there will be fear.

—There is always reassurance. God promises his presence ("The Lord is with you, Mighty Warrior!" an angel assures Gideon who had certainly never been addressed by that title before). God also promises to give whatever gifts are needed to fulfill his assignment ("I will help you to speak, and teach you what to say" he tells a stuttering Moses).

—There is always a decision. Sometimes, as with Moses and Gideon, people say yes to God's call. Sometimes, as with the ten frightened spies or the rich young ruler who spoke with Jesus, they say no. But always people must decide.

—There is always a changed life. Those who say yes to God's call don't walk the walk perfectly—not by a long shot. But because they say yes to God, they learn and grow even from their failures. And they become part of his actions to redeem the world.

Those who say no are changed too. They become a little harder, a little more resistant to his calling, a little more likely to say no the next time. Whatever the decision, it always changes a life—and it changes the world that little life touches.

I believe that this pattern from Scripture continues today. I believe that there is some aspect of your life in which God is calling you to walk with and to him, and that when we say yes to his calling, it sets in motion a divine dynamic far beyond merely human power. Maybe it has to do with your work or a relational risk or a gift you could develop or resources you could give. Probably it will involve facing your deepest fear. Certainly it will go to the core of who you are and what you do.

So, together in this book we are going to learn the skills essential to "water-walking": discerning God's call, transcending fear, risking faith, managing failure, trusting God. My hope is that you don't simply read this book, but that it prompts you to say yes to God.

So I want to invite you to go for a walk. On the water.

Just remember one thing: If you want to walk on water, you've got to get out of the boat.

CHAPTER 1

On Water-Walking

*It's not the critic who counts; not the man who points
out how the strong man stumbles, or where the doer
of deeds could have done better. The credit belongs
to the man who is actually in the arena ... who, at
best, knows in the end the triumph of great achievement, and who, at the worst, if he fails, at least fails
while daring greatly. So that his place will never be
with those cold timid souls who know neither victory
or defeat.*

Theodore Roosevelt

Some years ago my wife arranged for us to ride in a hot-air balloon as
a birthday gift. We went to the field where the balloons ascended and
got into a little basket with one other couple. We introduced ourselves
and swapped vocational information. Then our pilot began the ascent.
The day had just dawned—clear, crisp, cloudless. We could see the
entire Canejo Valley, from craggy canyons to the Pacific Ocean. It was
scenic, inspiring, and majestic.

But I also experienced one emotion I had not anticipated. Want
to guess?

Fear.

I had always thought those baskets went about chest high, but this
one only came up to our knees. One good lurch would be enough to
throw someone over the side. So I held on with grim determination
and white knuckles.

I looked over at my wife, who does not care for heights at all, and relaxed a bit, knowing there was someone in the basket more tense than I was. I could tell, because she would not move—at all. During part of our flight there was a horse ranch on the ground directly behind her. I pointed it out because she loves horses, and, without turning around or even pivoting her head, she simply rolled her eyes back as far as she could and said, "Yes, it's beautiful."

About this time I decided I'd like to get to know the kid who was flying this balloon. I realized that I could try to psyche myself up into believing everything would be fine, but the truth was we had placed our lives and destinies in the hands of the pilot. Everything depended on his character and competence.

I asked him what he did for a living and how he got started flying hot-air balloons. I was hoping for his former job to be one full of responsibilities—a neurosurgeon, perhaps, an astronaut who missed going up into space.

I knew we were in trouble when his response to me began, "Dude, it's like this...."

He did not even have a job! He mostly surfed.

He said the reason he got started flying hot-air balloons was that he had been driving around in his pickup when he'd had too much to drink, crashed the truck, and badly injured his brother. His brother still couldn't get around too well, so watching hot-air balloons gave him something to do.

"By the way," he added, "if things get a little choppy on the way down, don't be surprised. I've never flown this particular balloon before, and I'm not sure how it's going to handle the descent."

My wife looked over at me and said, "You mean to tell me we are a thousand feet up in the air with an unemployed surfer who started flying hot-air balloons because he got drunk, crashed a pickup, injured his brother, and has never been in this one before and doesn't know how to bring it down?"

Then the wife of the other couple looked at me and spoke—the only words either of them were to utter throughout the entire flight.

You're a pastor. Do something religious.

So I took an offering.

The great question at a moment like that is, *Can I trust the pilot?*

I could try telling myself that everything would turn out okay. Facing the flight with a positive attitude would certainly make it a more pleasant journey. But the journey would be over soon. And the real issue concerned the dude who was flying this thing. Were his character and competence such that I could confidently place my destiny in his hands?

Or, was it time to do something religious?

Every day you and I take another leg of our journey in this giant balloon that's whirling around a vast universe. We only get one trip. I long to take it with an enormous spirit of adventure and risk—and I'll bet you do, too.

But it's a pretty uncertain ride sometimes. I wish the walls to my basket went up a little higher. I wish the balloon was a little thicker. I wonder how my little ride will end up. I'm not sure how it will handle on the way down.

I can try to psyche myself up for taking chances and believing everything will turn out okay. But the real question is, Is there somebody piloting this thing? And are his character and competence such that he can be trusted? Because if they're not, I don't want to take a chance. My story, like every human story, is, at least in part, the struggle between faith and fear.

Because of this, I have found myself drawn for many years to the story of Peter getting out of the boat and walking on the water with Christ. It is one of the greatest pictures of extreme discipleship in Scripture. In the following chapters we will take a close look at each detail of this story for what it teaches us about water-walking. But for the rest of this chapter, let's get an aerial overview. What goes into the making of a water-walker?

Water-Walkers Recognize God's Presence

Peter and his friends got into a little boat one afternoon to cross the Sea of Galilee. Jesus wanted to be alone, so they were boating without him. Peter didn't mind—he'd been on boats his whole life. He liked them.

But this time a storm blew in. Not a minor squall, either. The gospel of Matthew says the boat was "tormented" by the waves. It was so violent that the only thing the disciples could do was to keep the boat upright. They wished the sides were a little higher and the wood a little thicker. By 3:00 A.M. I would imagine the disciples weren't worried about making it to the other side—they just wanted to stay alive.

Then one of the disciples noticed a shadow moving toward them on the water. As it got closer, it became apparent that it was the figure of a human being—walking on the water.

Take a moment to let that image sink in. The disciples were in distress, and the very person who was able to help them was approaching them. Only he wasn't in the boat and the disciples didn't recognize him. Amazingly enough, being boatless didn't seem to slow Jesus down at all.

But the disciples were convinced he was a ghost, so they were terrified and cried out in fear. In hindsight, we may wonder how they could have failed to know it was Jesus. Who else would it be? But Matthew wants us to know that sometimes it takes eyes of faith to recognize when Jesus is around. Often in the middle of the storm, tormented by waves of disappointment and doubt, we are no better at recognizing his presence than they were.

Let's probe deeper for a moment. What was Jesus up to, walking around on the lake at three o'clock in the morning?

What was Jesus up to, walking around on the lake at three o'clock in the morning?

David Garland finds a clue in Mark's version of this story. Mark tells us that Jesus "intended to pass them by" on the water, but when they saw him walking on the lake, they thought it was a ghost. Why did Jesus want to "pass them by"? Did he decide to race them? Did he want to impress them with a really neat trick?

Garland points out that the verb *parerchomai* ("to pass by") is used in the Greek translation of the Old Testament as a technical term to refer to a theophany—those defining moments when God made "striking and temporary appearances in the earthly realm to a select individual or group for the purpose of communicating a message."

God put Moses in a cleft in a rock so Moses could see "'while my glory *passes by.*'... The LORD passed before him."

God told Elijah to stand on the mountain "for the LORD is about to *pass by.*"

There is a pattern to these stories. In each case God had to get people's attention—through a burning bush, or wind and fire, or walking on the water. With each person God was going to call them to do something extraordinary. In each situation the person that God called felt afraid. But every time that people said "yes" to their calling, they experienced the power of God in their lives.

So when Jesus came to the disciples on the water intending "to pass them by," he was not just doing a neat magic trick. He was revealing his divine presence and power. Only God can do such a thing: "He alone ... treads on the waves of the sea."

It is interesting that the disciples entered the boat in the first place at Jesus' command. They would have to learn—as do we—that obedience is no guarantee of being spared adversity. But now that the storm had their full attention, Jesus decided it was time the disciples got to know a little bit more about the guy who was piloting this thing. *It's like this, dudes,* he reassured them. *You can trust me. You know my character and my competence. You can safely place your destiny in my hand. Take courage. It's me.*

They didn't fully grasp it yet, but God was visiting them in the water-walking flesh.

Matthew wants his readers to know that Jesus often comes when least expected—3:00 A.M., in the middle of a storm. Dale Bruner notes that, "according to the Holy Scriptures, human extremity is the frequent meeting place with God." Those divinely appointed defining moments will come to you and me. He still asks his followers to do extraordinary things. And if you're not looking for him, you just might miss him.

> If you're not looking for him, you just might miss him.

Twelve disciples sat in the boat, and we don't know how eleven of them responded to that voice. Perhaps with confusion, wonder, disbelief, or a little bit of each.

But one of them, Peter, was about to become a water-walker. He recognized that God was present—even in the most unlikely place. He realized that this was an extraordinary opportunity for spiritual adventure and growth. So he got an idea.

He decided to do something religious.

Water-Walkers Discern Between Faith and Foolishness

Peter blurted out to the water-walker, "If it is you, command me to come to you on the water." Why does Matthew include this detail? Why doesn't Peter just plunge into the water? I think it's for a very important reason. This is not just a story about risk-taking; it is primarily a story about *obedience*. That means I will have to discern between an authentic call from God and what might simply be a foolish impulse on my part. Courage alone is not enough; it must be accompanied by wisdom and discernment.

Matthew is not glorifying risk-taking for its own sake. Jesus is not looking for bungee jumping, hang-gliding, day-trading, tornado-chasing Pinto drivers. Water-walking is not something Peter does for recreational purposes. This is not a story about extreme sports. It's about *extreme discipleship*. This means that before Peter gets out of the boat, he had better make sure Jesus thinks it's a good idea. So he asks for clarity, "If it is you, command me...."

And in the darkness, I think Jesus smiled. Maybe he laughed. Because one person in the boat got it. Peter had some inkling of what it is that the Master is doing. Not only that, Peter had enough faith to believe that he too could share the adventure. He decided he wanted to be part of history's original water-walk. *Command me*.

Water-Walkers Get Out of the Boat

Before we go any further, I want you to put yourself in the story. Picture in your mind how violent the storm must have been if it was strong enough to keep seasoned professionals struggling just to avoid being capsized. Imagine the size of the waves, the strength of the wind, the darkness of this night—and no Dramamine! These were the conditions under which Peter was going to get out of the boat.

It would be tough enough to try to walk on the water when the water is calm, the sun is bright, and the air is still. Imagine trying to do it when the waves are crashing, the wind is at gale force, and it's three o'clock in the morning—and you're terrified.

Put yourself in Peter's place for a moment. You have a sudden insight into what Jesus is doing—the Lord is passing by. He's inviting you to go on the adventure of your life. But at the same time, you're scared to death. What would you choose—the water or the boat?

The boat is safe, secure, and comfortable.

On the other hand, the water is rough. The waves are high. The wind is strong. There's a storm out there. And if you get out of the boat—whatever your boat might happen to be—there's a good chance you might sink.

But if you don't get out of the boat, there's a guaranteed certainty that you will never walk on the water. This is an immutable law of nature.

If you want to walk on the water, you've got to get out of the boat.

I believe there is something—Someone—inside us who tells us there is more to life than sitting in the boat. You were made for something more than merely avoiding failure. There is something inside you that wants to walk on the water—to leave the comfort of routine existence and abandon yourself to the high adventure of following God.

So let me ask you a very important question: *What's your boat?*

Your boat is whatever represents safety and security to you apart from God himself. Your boat is whatever you are tempted to put your trust in, especially when life gets a little stormy. Your boat is whatever keeps you so comfortable that you don't want to give it up even if it's keeping you from joining Jesus on the waves. Your boat is whatever pulls you away from the high adventure of extreme discipleship.

Want to know what your boat is? Your fear will tell you. Just ask yourself this: *What is it that most produces fear in me—especially when I think of leaving it behind and stepping out in faith?*

For David, it is his vocation. He has been a builder for thirty-five years; he is in his late fifties now. But he has been gnawed his whole life by a sense that God was calling him into church ministry. He has quieted his conscience by giving away a lot of money and doing many good things, but he can't shake off the haunting fear that he has missed his calling. And he's afraid that perhaps it's too late.

For Kathy, it is a relationship. She has been involved for years with a man whose commitment to her is ambivalent at best. He is sending her signals that everyone else can read clearly; he never initiates the language of affection, avoids talking about their future, and creates as much distance from her as possible. But she never pursues discovering his true feelings—she's too frightened. She doesn't believe she could handle losing him. Her boat is pretty shaky. But she's too scared to leave.

Ralph is the pastor of a church he neither fits nor loves. It is filled with division and petty squabbling. Rather than speaking prophetic truth or leading with clear vision, he finds himself constantly trying to placate angry attendees and keep the peace. He does not like the church; he resents and fears it. But it's his boat. If he leaves it, it will only be to find himself in another just like it.

Doug's boat is secrecy. He is addicted to pornography. It is a mild addiction, or so he tells himself, mostly adult movies on business trips and occasional sprees on the internet. Nothing that has cost him a job or a marriage—so far. But no one knows. He's afraid to admit it. He's afraid to get help. Secrecy is killing him. But it's his boat.

Kim's boat is her dad. She raises her children, keeps her house, and pursues a career designed to make her dad happy. The irony is that her dad is not happy, and nothing she can do will ever be enough to please him. But the thought of crossing him terrifies her. His approval is a pretty leaky vessel. But it's her boat.

Maybe your boat is success. That was the case for the rich young ruler in the Bible. Jesus asked him to get out of the boat ("sell all that you have, give the money to the poor, and come and follow me") but he decided not to. He had a very nice boat. A yacht. It handled well, and he liked it too much to give it up.

I wonder sometimes if he ever thought about that encounter with Jesus when he reached the end of his life—when he was an old man and his bank account, stock portfolio, and trophy case were full. Did he ever remember the day a carpenter's son called him to risk the whole thing for one wild bet on the kingdom of God—and he said no?

What is your boat? In what area of your life are you shrinking back from fully and courageously trusting God? Fear will tell you what your boat is. Leaving it may be the hardest thing you ever do.

But if you want to walk on the water, you've got to get out of the boat.

Water-Walkers Expect Problems

So Peter goes to the side of the boat. The other disciples are watching closely. They have seen Peter shoot off his mouth before—a lot. They wonder how far he'll take this thing.

He puts one foot over the side, carefully gripping the edge of the boat. Then the other foot. He's holding on with grim determination and white knuckles.

Then he does something religious—he lets go. He abandons himself utterly to the power of Jesus. And suddenly, for the first time in history, an ordinary human being is walking on the water.

For a while it's as if only Peter and Jesus are present on the water. Peter is beaming with delight. Jesus is thrilled with his student. *Like master, like disciple.*

Then it happens. Peter "saw the wind."

Reality sets in, and Peter asks himself, *What was I thinking?* He realized he was on the water in the middle of a storm with no boat beneath him—and he was terrified. Nothing has really changed, though. The storm should have come as no surprise—it's been there all along. What has really taken place is that Peter's focus has shifted from the Savior to the storm.

> The storm should have come as no surprise— it's been there all along.

We all know what it is to "see the wind." You begin a new adventure full of hope. Maybe it's a new job; maybe you're testing an area of spiritual giftedness; maybe you're trying to serve God in a new way. At the beginning you are full of faith—it's blue skies.

Then reality sets in. Setbacks. Opposition. Unexpected obstacles. You see the wind. It should be expected—the world's a pretty stormy place. But somehow trouble still has the power to catch us by surprise.

Because of the wind, some people decide never to leave the boat. If you get out of the boat, you will face the wind and the storm out there. But you might as well know now, there is no guarantee that life in the boat is going to be any safer.

Eileen Guder wrote,

> You can live on bland food so as to avoid an ulcer, drink no tea, coffee or other stimulants in the name of health, go to bed early, stay away from night life, avoid all controversial subjects so as never to give offense, mind your own business, avoid involvement in other people's problems, spend money only on necessities and save all you can.
>
> You can still break your neck in the bath tub, and it will serve you right.

Larry Laudan, a philosopher of science, has spent the last decade studying risk-management. He writes of how we live in a society so fear-driven that we suffer from what he calls *risk-lock*—a condition which, like gridlock, leaves us unable to do anything or go anywhere. He summarizes literature on risk management in nineteen principles. The first principle is the simplest: *Everything is risky*. If you're looking for absolute safety, you chose the wrong species. You can stay home in bed—but that may make you one of the half-million Americans who require emergency room treatment each year for injuries sustained while falling out of bed. You can cover your windows—but that may make you one of the ten people a year who accidentally hang themselves on the cords of their venetian blinds. You can hide your money in a mattress—but that may make you one of tens of thousands of the people who go to the emergency room each year because of wounds caused by handling money—everything from paper cuts to (for the wealthy) hernias.

If you step up to the plate, you may strike out. The greatest hitters in the world fail two times out of three.

But it you don't step up to the plate, you will never know the glory of what it is to hit a home run. There is danger in getting out of the boat. But there is danger in staying in it as well. If you live in the boat—whatever your boat happens to be—you will eventually die of boredom and stagnation. *Everything is risky*.

Water-Walkers Accept Fear as the Price of Growth

Now we come to a part of the story you may not like very much. I don't care for it much myself. The choice to follow Jesus—the choice to grow—is the choice for the constant recurrence of fear. You've got to get out of the boat a little every day.

Let me explain. The disciples get into the boat, face the storm, see the water-walker, and are afraid. "Don't be afraid," Jesus says. Peter then girds up his loins, asks permission to go overboard, sees the wind, and is afraid all over again. "Don't be afraid," Jesus says. Do you think that's the last time in his life Peter will experience fear?

Here is a deep truth about water-walking: *The fear will never go away.* Why? Because each time I want to grow, it will involve going into new territory, taking on new challenges. And each time I do that, I will experience fear again. As Susan Jeffers writes, "The fear will never go away, as long as I continue to grow."

Never! Isn't that great news? Now you can give up trying to make fear go away. Fear and growth go together like macaroni and cheese. It's a package deal. The decision to grow always involves a choice between risk and comfort. This means that to be a follower of Jesus you must renounce comfort as the ultimate value of your life. And that's sobering news to most of us, because we're into comfort. Theologian Karl Barth said that comfort is one of the great siren calls of our age.

Would you like to guess the name of the best-selling chair in America?

La-Z-Boy.

Not Risk-E-Boy.

Not Work-R-Boy.

La-Z-Boy. We want to immerse ourselves in comfort. We have developed a whole language around this. People say, "I want to go home and *veg out*—make myself as much like vegetation as humanly possible, preferably in front of a television set."

We have a name for people who do this in front of TV, too: couch potatoes. Couch potatoes in their La-Z-Boys.

The eleven disciples could be called "boat potatoes." They didn't mind watching, but they didn't want to actually *do* anything.

Millions of people in churches these days could be called "pew potatoes." They want some of the comfort associated with spirituality, but they don't want the risk and challenge that go along with actually following Jesus. Yet Jesus is still looking for people who will get out of the boat. He is looking for someone who will say, if you'll pardon the expression, "I may be small potatoes, Lord, but this spud's for you."

And as we will see in this book, both choices—risk and comfort—tend to grow into a habit. Each time you get out of the boat, you become a little more likely to get out the next time. It's not that the fear goes away, but that you get used to living with fear. You realize that it does not have the power to destroy you.

On the other hand, every time you resist that voice, every time you choose to stay in the boat rather than heed its call, the voice gets a little quieter in you. Then at last you don't hear its call at all.

Water-Walkers Master Failure Management

As a result of seeing the wind and giving in to fear, Peter began to sink into the water. So here is the question: Did Peter fail? Before I offer an answer, let me make an observation about failure, because in this book we talk a lot about it.

Failure is not an event, but rather a *judgment* about an event. Failure is not something that happens to us or a label we attach to things. It is a way we think about outcomes.

Before Jonas Salk developed a vaccine for polio that finally worked, he tried two hundred unsuccessful ones. Somebody asked him, "How did it feel to fail two hundred times?"

"I never failed two hundred times in my life," Salk replied. "I was taught not to use the word 'failure.' I just discovered two hundred ways how not to vaccinate for polio."

Somebody once asked Winston Churchill what most prepared him to risk political suicide by speaking out against Hitler during the years of appeasement in the mid–1930s, then to lead Great Britain against Nazi Germany. Churchill said it was the time he had to repeat a grade in elementary school.

"You mean you failed a year in grade school?" he was asked.

"I never failed anything in my life. I was given a second opportunity to get it right."

Jonas Salk made two hundred unsuccessful attempts to create a polio vaccine. *Was Jonas Salk a failure?*

Winston Churchill repeated a grade in elementary school. *Was Winston Churchill a failure?*

I grew up in northern Illinois and have rooted for the Chicago Cubs my entire life. As of this writing, the Cubs have not been in the World Series for fifty-four years. In fact, they have not won the World Series for ninety years. *Are the Chicago Cubs a failure?*

Okay, bad example.

Did Peter fail?

Well, I suppose in a way he did. His faith wasn't strong enough. His doubts were stronger. "He saw the wind." He took his eyes off of where they should have been. He sank. He failed.

But here is what I think. *I think there were eleven bigger failures sitting in the boat.* They failed quietly. They failed privately. Their failure went unnoticed, unobserved, uncriticized. Only Peter knew the shame of public failure.

But only Peter knew two other things as well. Only Peter knew the glory of walking on the water. He alone knew what it was to attempt to do what he was not capable of doing on his own, then feeling the euphoria of being empowered by God to actually do it.

> **Peter failed. But I think there were eleven bigger failures sitting in the boat.**

Once you walk on the water, you never forget it—not for the rest of your life. I think Peter carried that joyous moment with him to his grave.

And only Peter knew the glory of being lifted up by Jesus in a moment of desperate need. Peter knew, in a way the others could not, that when he sank, Jesus would be wholly adequate to save him. He had a shared moment, a shared connection, a shared trust in Jesus that none of the others had.

They couldn't, because they didn't even get out of the boat. The worst failure is not to sink in the waves. The worst failure is to never get out of the boat.

Water-Walkers See Failure as an Opportunity to Grow

As soon as Peter asks for help, Jesus is there. He helps Peter physically by pulling him from the water. But he also helps Peter grow by pinpointing the problem: "You of little faith, why did you doubt?"

I don't think Jesus is being harsh or critical here. In fact, one detail I love about this story is that Jesus makes this comment to Peter when they are alone on the water. The text says it is only after this comment that they got into the boat. It may be that Jesus—like any good mentor—did not want to embarrass Peter in front of the other disciples. So in the privacy and safety of his strong right hand, he gently helps Peter locate the source of his problem.

The problem was quite clear: Whether Peter sank or water-walked depended on whether he focused on the storm or on Jesus. But now he understood his dependence on faith much more deeply than he would have if he had never left the boat. It was his willingness to risk failure that helped him to grow.

Even more than we hate to fail, we hate for other people to see us fail. If I had been Peter, I would have been tempted to try to cover up what happened when I got back into the boat with the other disciples: *Yes—water-walking was great for a while. But then I got hot and thought how good it would feel to go for a quick swim. . . .*

> **It was Peter's willingness to risk failure that helped him to grow.**

Because Peter puts himself in a position to *fail*, he also puts himself in a position to *grow*. Failure is an indispensable, irreplaceable part of learning and growth. Here is the principle involved: Failure does not shape you; the way you *respond* to failure shapes you.

Sir Edmund Hillary made several unsuccessful attempts at scaling Mount Everest before he finally succeeded. After one attempt he stood at the base of the giant mountain and shook his fist at it. "I'll defeat you yet," he said in defiance. "Because you're as big as you're going to get—but *I'm still growing.*"

Every time Hillary climbed, he failed. And every time he failed, he learned. And every time he learned, he grew and tried again. And one day he didn't fail.

Water-Walkers Learn to Wait on the Lord

This story about risk is also a story about waiting. The disciples had to wait in the storm until the fourth watch of the night before Jesus came to them. Even then, it's not until the very end of the passage that the disciples finally get what they were hoping for—relief from the storm. Why couldn't Jesus have made the wind die down *before* Peter got out of the boat?

Maybe because they—like us—needed to learn something about waiting.

We have to learn to wait on the Lord to receive power to walk on the water. We have to wait for the Lord to make the storm disappear.

In some ways, "waiting on the Lord" is the hardest part of trusting. It is not the same as "waiting around." It is putting yourself with utter vulnerability in his hands.

All my life I have loved to talk. When I was not yet two years old, I memorized my sister's part in a Sunday school pageant and demanded to be allowed to say it as well. (So I'm told; I don't personally remember this at all.) In surveys, fear of public speaking is consistently named as most peoples' number one fear—even ahead of death. I never understood this, because early in life it became a source of joy to me.

When I first began to preach and teach, I found it a deeply moving experience. I had some sense that this is what I was made to do. It was part of my calling.

One Sunday early on, I was about ten minutes into the message when I started getting very warm and dizzy. The next thing I knew, I was lying on the ground with several anxious faces checking to see if I was all right. I had fainted in the middle of a sermon.

After a year of studying abroad, I returned to the same church. The very next time I went to preach, the same thing happened. I went down ten minutes into the talk.

And unfortunately for me, this was a Baptist church, not a charismatic one. It wasn't the kind of church where you get credit for this sort of thing. No one interpreted it as being "slain in the Spirit." When you're a Baptist, fainting is just fainting. It did increase attendance for a while, somewhat like the possibility of an accident at the Indy 500—

25

people don't exactly hope that one will happen, but they don't want to miss it if it does.

But it was a painful thing for me. I did not understand why this was going on. I had some sense that preaching was what I was called to do—what I loved to do. But I did not know whether I could do it. I did know, however, that a person can't preach if it means fainting on a regular basis. It makes others nervous.

Well-meaning people offered all kinds of advice: "You just need to try really hard to relax and trust more." Ever try *really hard* to relax?

I was scheduled to preach quite often that summer. The senior pastor of the church, who was on sabbatical, offered to take me off the hook by getting some replacements.

But somehow I knew that if I didn't get up and speak that next weekend, it wasn't going to get any easier. I asked God to take away the fear of its happening again. He didn't. I remembered the passage from Isaiah—

> Even youths will faint and be weary,
> and the young will fall exhausted;
> but those who wait for the LORD
> shall renew their strength.

So I got up and preached. Not a great sermon by any stretch of the imagination, although the congregation was alarmingly attentive. It was nothing dramatic; it is done every Sunday by thousands of men and women around the world. But I made it to the end, which was a personal triumph.

I began to learn something about what it means to "wait on the Lord." It has been sixteen years since the last time I fainted while preaching, but every now and then I will have a little flash of what it felt like to be nervous enough to faint. It still doesn't feel good to think about it, and I am still waiting for the apprehension to go away altogether—for the wind to die down. It reminds me of my own finitude and dependence. And each time I preach, it is, at least in part, an exercise in waiting on God.

But if I don't preach, I will never again know the exhilaration of doing what I believe God has called me to do. I will not be faithful to what I understand to be my calling. So I am learning to wait.

On Water-Walking

Water-Walking Brings a Deeper Connection with God

Jesus is still looking for people who will get out of the boat. Why risk it? I believe there are many reasons:

—It is the only way to real growth.
—It is the way true faith develops.
—It is the alternative to boredom and stagnation that causes people to wither up and die.
—It is part of discovering and obeying your calling.

I believe there are many good reasons to get out of the boat. But there is one that trumps them all: *The water is where Jesus is*. The water may be dark, wet, and dangerous. But Jesus is not in the boat. The main reason Peter got out of the boat is that he wanted to be where Jesus was. Matthew keeps referring to this reality. Peter's request is, "Lord, if it's you, command me to *come to you*." Then Peter got out of the boat *"and came toward Jesus."*

Because Peter did this, both he and his friends came to a deeper understanding of their Master than ever before. They came to see more than ever that they could place their destinies in his hands with confidence. *"It's like this, dudes. . . ."*

They understood that the One in their boat was the One alone who treads the waves of the seas—and they worshiped him.

How about you? When was the last time you got out of the boat?

I believe that God's general method for growing a deep, adventuresome faith in us is by asking us to get out of the boat. More than hearing a great talk, or reading a great book, God uses real-world challenges to develop our ability to trust in him.

We tend to seek a world of comfort. We try to construct manageable lives with some security and predictability to maintain the illusion that we are in control.

Then God "passes us by" and shakes everything up. The call to get out of the boat involves crisis, opportunity, often failure, generally fear, sometimes suffering, always the calling to a task too big for us. But there is no other way to grow faith and to partner with God.

Maybe there was a time in your life when you were walking on the water on a regular basis. A time when your heart was much like Peter's:

27

"Command me. Tell me to come to you." A time when you would risk sharing your faith even if it meant rejection; giving, even if it meant sacrifice; serving, even if it meant the possibility of failure. Sometimes you sank. Sometimes you soared. But you lived on the edge of faith.

Maybe now, though, you haven't been out of the boat in a long time. You may have a very nice boat, with padded deck chairs and stabilizers so you never get seasick in the storm. You may have gotten quite comfortable sitting in your boat.

But the Lord is passing by! Jesus is still looking for people who will get out of the boat. I don't know what this means for you. If you get out of your boat—whatever your boat happens to be—you will have problems. There is a storm out there, and your faith will not be perfect. Risk always holds the possibility of failure.

> When you fail … Jesus will be there to pick you up. You will not fail alone.

But if you get out, I believe two things will happen. The first is that when you fail—and you will fail sometimes—Jesus will be there to pick you up. You will not fail alone. You will find that he is still wholly adequate to save.

And the other thing is, every once in a while you will walk on the water.

So do something religious.

Get out of the boat.

GETTING OUT OF THE BOAT

1. What's your boat? Where is fear or comfort keeping you from trusting God?
2. In what area do you need discernment to know if you're really being called to get out of the boat?
3. What's one risk you can take in your life that could help your faith to grow:

   ❏ Stand up for a value you believe in during a tough conversation?
   ❏ Express affection even though it may be hard for you?
   ❏ Take on a challenge that you know will stretch you?

4. What's one failure from your past that haunts you? What trusted friend can you share it with as a step in robbing it of its power?
5. Where are you in relation to Jesus these days?

❏ Huddled in the boat with a life preserver and the seat belt on
❏ One leg in, one leg out
❏ I'm walking on the water—and loving it
❏ I'm out of the boat—but the wind looks pretty bad

So Peter got out of the boat, started walking on the water, and came toward Jesus.

Matthew 14:29

Boat Potatoes

The dismal company whose lives knew neither praise nor infamy; who against God rebelled not, nor to Him were faithful, but to self alone were true.

Dante Alighieri

Sometime after Florence, my paternal grandmother, died, my grandfather called my mother with an unusual offer.

"Kathy," he said, in his heavy Swedish accent. "I was going through some of Florence's things in the attic when I came across a box of old dishes. I was going to get rid of them, but I noticed that they're blue—your favorite color. Why don't you take a look at them, and if you want them, they're yours; otherwise, I'll give them to the Salvation Army."

So my mother went through the attic, expecting to find some run-of-the-mill dinnerware. Instead, when she opened the box, she was looking at some of the most exquisite china she had ever seen. Each plate had been individually painted with a pattern of forget-me-nots. The cups were inlaid mother-of-pearl. The dishes and cups were rimmed with gold. The plates had been handcrafted in a Bavarian factory that was destroyed during the Second World War, so they were literally irreplaceable.

Yet my mother had been in the family for twenty years, and she had never seen this china before. She asked my father about it. He had grown up in the family—and he had never seen it, either.

Eventually they found out from some older family members the story of the china. When Florence was very young, she was given this china over a period of years. They were not a wealthy family, and the china was quite valuable, so she only got a piece at a time for gifts—confirmation, graduation, or a birthday.

Why had my parents never seen it? To know that, you have to know something about the character of Swedes. We are a cautious kind of people. We don't roll the dice easily. For instance, my two great-aunts lived for eighty years in a beautiful Victorian home built by my great-grandfather in the 1800s. The most beautiful room in the house was a parlor. It was generally reserved for very special guests. No guest that special ever came to the house, so the parlor didn't get used much.

Whenever Florence received a piece of china—because it was so valuable, because if it was used it might get broken—she would wrap it very carefully in tissue, put it in a box, and store it in the attic for a very special occasion. No occasion that special ever came along. So my grandmother went to her grave with the greatest gift of her life unopened and unused.

Then my mother was given the dishes. She uses them promiscuously—every chance she has. They have finally made it out of the box.

The Two Ways

Anytime a gift is given, the recipient must choose to respond in one of two ways. The first way says, *This gift is so valuable it can't be risked.* Those who follow the first way realize that when the gift is brought out of the box and into the open, things may not always go well. The gift may be poorly used sometimes. It may not always be admired by others the way we want. It may even get broken. Taking the gift out of the box is always a risk.

The second way says, *This gift is so valuable it must be risked.* Those who follow the second way understand that if the gift is not brought out of the box, it will never be used at all. To leave the gift in the box is to thwart the desire of the giver. *There is no tragedy like the tragedy of the unopened gift.*

You, too, have been given a gift. We will look in the next chapter at how to discover what's inside your box—how to discern what God has gifted you and called you to do. But for now I want to invite you to do a bit of ruthless self-assessment. Along with the gift you have been given a choice—whether or not you will open and use what was given to you. Is your life following the first way or the second?

Peter chose the second way. Dale Bruner writes, "It is important to see that Peter did not ask Jesus for a *promise*—e.g., 'Lord, promise me I won't sink'—but specifically for a *command*: 'Lord, if it is you, *command* me.'" Peter didn't ask for a guarantee, just an opportunity.

The disciples who stayed in the boat were, like my grandmother, followers of the first way. They did not want to risk brokenness or failure. They treasured safety over growth. The Lord wanted to "pass them by"—to reveal himself in his adventuresome splendor—not to bypass them! The ultimate adventure of faith was something they were content to watch from the sidelines. They didn't want to be passed by, just passed up. Let them stand for all who ask not for a command but a promise, who seek not a mission but a guarantee.

They understood the cost of getting out of the boat. They were very much aware of the pain of potential failure, embarrassment, inadequacy, criticism, and perhaps even loss of life.

But what they were not so aware of was another price—the cost of staying in the boat.

The High Cost of Being a Boat Potato

If I had to name, in a single word, the price you pay for being a boat potato, I think the word written on the price tag would read *growth*.

There are few things that attract us more than growth. We were made to grow, and we love to be around growth. We plant gardens; we set aside forest preserves, we wait for the first blade of grass to come up in spring; we want to watch the miracle of *growth*.

We love to watch newborns grow. Our firstborn tripled her weight during her initial year of life. I figured it out—if she kept going at that rate, she'd weigh 486 pounds by the time she was four.

Think about the excitement of parents whose child says his first word. Yesterday he could only cry or babble—today he has joined the ranks of those who speak. His parents are excited.

They will regret it sometimes in the days to come, when the talk seems incessant, but today they are excited. They are watching the miracle of *growth*.

Consider the sense of fulfillment in the leaders of a company that is expanding, achieving its mission, giving vocational opportunities to men and women who yesterday didn't have any. They are watching the miracle of *growth*.

Watch the ecstasy of a sixteen-year-old who earns a driver's license. Yesterday she was just a pedestrian. Today she is a danger to everyone she knows. She's growing!

On the other hand, there are few things sadder than stagnation.

Not many people plan a vacation to the Dead Sea.

Watch a marriage that was begun with hope and dreams, but has now plateaued, where affections have cooled and intimacy has faded. Rather than name the problem, face their pain, and ask for help, the couple resign themselves to a life of mediocrity, living together as intimate strangers.

See a middle-aged man who spends his nights sitting in front of a television set watching whatever sport happens to be on cable. He was once all fired up with bright plans for the future and strong yearnings to make his mark on this world. But somewhere along the line all the fire went out, and he settled for comfort. His dreams were sacrificed to a La-Z-Boy and flickering images on a screen. He is the story of unrealized potential.

This is a way that leads to stagnation—unrealized potential, unfilled longings. It leads to a sense that I'm not living *my* life; the one I was supposed to live. It leads to boredom, to what Gregg Levoy calls the common cold of the soul.

> To sinful patterns of behavior that never get confronted and
>   changed,
> Abilities and gifts that never get cultivated and deployed—
> Until weeks become months
> And months turn into years,
> And one day you're looking back on a life of
> Deep intimate gut-wrenchingly honest conversations you
>   never had;

Great bold prayers you never prayed,
Exhilarating risks you never took,
Sacrificial gifts you never offered
Lives you never touched,
And you're sitting in a recliner with a shriveled soul,
And forgotten dreams,
And you realize there was a world of desperate need,
And a great God calling you to be part of something bigger
    than yourself—
You see the person you could have become but did not;
You never followed your calling.
You never got out of the boat.

There is no tragedy like the tragedy of the unopened gift.

Garrison Keillor tells a story, called "A Day in the Life of Clarence Bunsen," about an older man who realizes the years have slipped away and his life has missed something. Clarence goes to see Father Emil at Our Lady of Perpetual Responsibility for some advice. Normally Clarence goes to the Lutheran church, but he wants a second opinion. When that doesn't help, he walks past his old school and climbs the hill overlooking Lake Wobegon, where he and his friends played as kids years ago.

While he is reflecting on his life, Clarence hears some kids coming up the path. For some strange reason he runs ahead of them and climbs an old tree he remembers from childhood. The kids stop right under his tree; they know he's around somewhere but don't think to look up. Clarence knew that if he dropped down on them or even yelled "Ha!" they would jump out of their shoes. He watches them, so full of excitement and life, and thinks to himself,

> *I wish I could be like that. I just seem to go through life with my eyes closed and my ears shut. People talk to me, and I don't even hear them. Whole days go by, and I can't remember what happened. The woman I've lived with for thirty-six years, if you asked me to describe her, I'd have to stop and think about it. It's like I've lived half my life waiting for my life to begin, thinking it's somewhere off in the future, and now I'm thinking about death all the time. It's time to live, to wake up and do something.*

And he jumped and yelled, "Hayee!"

Oh, those boys *exploded* out of there, like birds. And he yelled, "Haah!" And then he said, "Ouch! Ouch!"

They came back to where he was sitting and asked, "You all right, Uncle Clarence?"

He replied, "Yes. But go down and tell Mrs. Bunsen to bring the car up to the gravel road. I'll meet her by the mailbox."

He crawled a hundred yards over to the road. She picked him up and didn't ask what happened....

This is the tragedy of the unopened gift: *It's as if I've lived half my life waiting for life to begin, thinking it's somewhere off in the future.* As Thoreau hauntingly put it, "I did not wish to live what was not life.... I wanted to live deep and suck out all the marrow of life."

To serve as a wake-up call to potential boat potatoes, Jesus once told a story about a CEO and his three employees. Each of them was given a lavish opportunity. Like Florence. Like Peter. Like you and me. The Lord "intended to pass them by." Each of them had to decide what they would do.

Jesus teaches us three principles about the master—about God and the opportunity he offers us—we must understand if we are to embrace his gift.

He Is the Lord of the Gift

In those days there were no corporations as we know them. When the psalmist said, "Lift up your heads, O ye Gates," he wasn't thinking of Bill. Wealth was concentrated in a few rich households.

This is the story about one of them. The master gathers together three key employees and "entrusted his property to them."

Jesus talks about vast sums of money. The master gives his first servant five talents, the second servant two, and the third one. A talent was an expression for a sum of money worth in the neighborhood of fifteen years' wages. In that era, people lived from day to day, and to have accumulated one year's worth of wages was enormous wealth.

So the figures Jesus is throwing around here are staggering. This master would have been the Bill Gates of his village. A man of these means would certainly have had a labor force of many more than three men, so these three were in a remarkable position. He entrusts his treasure to them, then goes away.

As Kenneth Bailey writes in his great treatment of this parable, *Poet and Peasant*, it dawns on this first servant that this is an unbelievable opportunity. This is a chance for all of them to exercise initiative, use judgment, test their skills in the marketplace, and potentially rise to positions of greater responsibility. Most likely there would have been an implicit arrangement for them to share in profits as well.

This is an act of unprecedented trust and generosity. Vocationally, organizationally, and financially, the lord of the gift has given them the chance of a lifetime. This is their defining moment.

What will they do? The chance of a lifetime is not something to take lightly.

Nancy and I were married when I was still in graduate school. I wanted to go on the honeymoon of my dreams—to Hawaii, maybe. But because I had considerable financial liabilities and a severely restricted revenue stream (I worked part time at a Baptist church), I couldn't figure out how to finance it.

> The chance of a lifetime is not something to take lightly.

The only idea I came up with to get my hands on adequate capital was to go on a television game show. So I tried out for and was accepted as a contestant on a program called *Tic-Tac-Dough*, hosted by the very genial Wink Martindale.

It was a simple game, featuring a large tic-tac-toe board. Each box had a question from some randomly selected category, and if the contestant answered correctly, he or she got the X or O. The categories were switched after each answer.

The first game ended in a tie, as did the next three or four games. Each time that happened, the money would go into the jackpot, so before long it was worth many thousands of dollars. My opponent was a well-groomed lawyer with a tan that would make actor George Hamilton look like an albino. The lawyer lived in a house on the beach in Santa Monica and had won so many games that he was going for the bonus car. I was a Baptist preacher. I figured God had to be on my side. Finally, "George Hamilton" missed a question. All I needed was one right answer in one strategic box to get more money than I had ever seen.

I waited to see what category would come up with my whole wedded bliss on the line. I hoped it would be something I knew about. The Bible, maybe.

Then the category appeared: Mixed Drinks.

I could have chosen to answer the question in another square, keep my advantage, and win on the next question. But no—I wanted *this* square. I wanted to win *now*.

So the question popped up, "What is the drink made of ... two shots scotch, half-shot sweet vermouth?"

I told Wink, "I'm a pastor at a Baptist church. I'm in trouble if I get it wrong; I'm in trouble if I get it right."

We honeymooned in Wisconsin. I had encountered the chance of a lifetime time—and I blew it.

Jesus tells the story of the talents because the lord of the gift offers the chance of a lifetime. Up until now, the servants have simply been carrying out somebody else's orders. Their lives have been routine, predictable, and safe. They have had little authority, few resources, and limited responsibility. Then, with a single act, the master changes their destinies forever. If we were to listen to the first servant, he might say something like this:

> I thought my whole life was condemned to be routine. I had dreams, but couldn't pursue them; passions, but couldn't follow them; talents, but couldn't test them. I was never in a position to plan, take risks, or take initiative. My life was comfortable. I wasn't facing starvation, but I longed for something more. I wanted to make a difference.
>
> And just when I was ready to give up hope, the master did something I've never heard of anyone doing before. He called me into his office, looked at me from behind his desk with a twinkle in his eye, and entrusted a large portion of what belongs to him to me. I can't believe he has that kind of faith in me. I can't believe I have this opportunity. I feel like a thoroughbred that's been set free to run.

The first servant realizes he is getting the blue dishes. Wink Martindale has just offered him the chance of a lifetime. This explains a very important detail in this story, namely, why Jesus says the first employee responded "at once." The employee realizes it would be insane to let anything interfere. He responds at once because the thought of losing the chance of a lifetime is intolerable. He responds at once because if someone offers you a front row seat on the NASDAQ in a bull market, you don't ask them if maybe they were thinking about somebody else. Because if the phone rings, and it's model Cindy Crawford calling to ask you out for a date, you don't check to see if perhaps she dialed a wrong number. You just say yes. Quickly. The employee jumps at the opportunity before the master might reconsider or change his mind.

"At once" isn't so much a chronological detail as a statement about the recognition of reality. The first servant realizes that as long as he lives, he will never have another chance like this. He resolves that he will allow nothing to interfere with his seizing this opportunity. He will not be sidetracked or distracted. Jesus says this is how it is with anyone who grasps what God offers.

This part of the story has very important implications. The Lord of the Gift has entrusted his property to you and me. Everybody receives a gift. This is not a story where some are gifted and some are not. We are all called by God. We are all equipped and expected to contribute. Every gift is chosen by the master. I may like my gift, or I may not. I may torture myself by desiring what belongs to another, but it will do me no good. No one decides on his or her giftedness. I cannot pick out my own designer genes; I do not choose my family. The master chooses.

In place of the word *talent*, you might think about your life. Your mind. Your abilities. Your spiritual gifts. Your body. Your money. Your will.

In fact, we get the meaning of the word *talent* from this very story. He has been very generous, the lord of the gift. There are no no-talent people in his story. Not only that, God himself offers to partner with you in your life. He offers to guide you when you need wisdom, encourage you when you falter, pick you up when you sink, and forgive you when you stray. He offers us himself as the best gift of all.

All human beings, including you and me, give their lives to something. Between this day and your last day, you will give your life to something. The only question is, what will you give your life to? Will it be worthy?

The practical implication is, *I must come to prize and appreciate what the Lord of the Gift has given to me.*

Let me get more personal: You had better respond *at once.*

The opportunity to use whatever gifts you have in the service of the Lord of the Gift is the chance of a lifetime. But it will slip away from you unless you are very intentional. The time to respond is *at once.*

But the third servant fails to do this. He takes the greatest gift he will ever be given and buries it in a field. Why would he do such a thing? What would cause a human being to discard the chance of a lifetime?

I think I know something about this—I have some of that third servant in me. I remember when a classmate in college, one of my teammates on the tennis team, pointed out how something about me was making our relationship hard for him. It was so painful to hear this that, instead of embracing what he said and seeking his help to change, I just withdrew from the relationship. My inner attitude was, I'll become more distant and polite, and I hope you'll feel sorry you brought it up.

I lost a potential good friend—and a chance to grow, simply because I did not want to look carefully at the truth about myself. I preferred to bury it.

He Is the Lord of the Settled Account

This brings us to a second truth about the master. Somehow the third servant forgets a very important fact of life. He forgets that the lord of the gift is coming back. But the day comes. "After a long time, the master of those slaves came back and *settled accounts* with them."

There is an odd tendency in human beings to think we can worm or charm our way out of the consequences of our actions. Have you ever tried to finesse a police officer out of a traffic ticket? (*Honest, officer, I thought the speedometer was broken.*) Ever try to bluff your way with a lame excuse for being late to a teacher, boss, or spouse? This is a tendency that starts early in life.

Some years ago our son, who was about eight at the time, was having a generally squirrelly day. He was headed for trouble. I warned him that if he didn't settle down soon, he would face serious consequences involving the availability of Mr. Nintendo.

Then came a spill of Exxon Valdez proportions.

"Okay," I said, "you know the consequences."

This eight-year-old boy pulled a dollar bill out of his pocket, waved it in front of my nose, and suggested slyly, "Maybe Mr. Washington can change your mind."

There is one before whom we will all stand. He is loving, holy, gracious, and just, but he intends for us to understand that we really will give account to him of our lives. We will not be able to finesse our way around that throne; Mr. Washington will not change his mind.

> There is an odd tendency in human beings to think we can worm or charm our way out of the consequences of our actions.

It is amazing to me how often we forget this. So many people blame their refusal to get out of the boat on some external circumstance:

—I would develop my gifts more thoroughly, but I have a boss who stifles my initiative.

—I would pursue another job, but I need the money/security/familiarity of this one.

—I would grow in my capacity for intimacy, but my spouse isn't interested.

—I would devote myself more fully to spiritual growth, but I can't find the time.

—I would have realized more of my potential, but no one was ever interested in mentoring me.

We play what Susan Jeffers calls the "when-then game."

—"When I feel confident, I'll try using this gift."

—"When my boss is more supportive, I'll grow."

—"When my spouse is more cooperative, I'll work on being a better partner"

And we can wait our whole lives for a "when" that never comes.

I have been given a gift. It may not look like much—but it's mine. It's all I have. It was given to *me*.

The master is coming back. He's going to settle up—with all the CEOs, presidents, prime ministers, network anchors, mothers and fathers, plumbers, teachers, and you and me.

And he will ask, What did you do with what I gave you?

He will not ask your boss about this, or your spouse, or your parents, or friends—he will ask you.

A performance review is coming my way that will make every other performance review I've ever been through look pretty inconsequential. This is what the third servant forgot, which enabled him to justify—at least to himself—burying his gift with so little concern.

Here Jesus warns us about the primary reason that potential water-walkers turn into boat potatoes and how servants rationalize burying their gifts.

A Comparison

I find it intriguing that the man who buried his talent is the man who received only one talent. I wonder if comparing his one talent with the multiple talents of the other servants made him feel inadequate or insignificant. I wonder if he felt angry toward the other servants—or perhaps even toward the master. Maybe burying his talent was a passive way of getting even with the master for not giving him more.

In fact, I think this issue explains why Jesus has *three* servants in this story. Usually, in stories that involve pleasing versus unpleasing responses to God, Jesus simply has two characters—like the wise versus foolish builder, or the tax collector versus the publican. But here there are three characters, and Jesus (who is the master storyteller) needs them to establish a very important point.

In this story there are two variables. First, there are varying amounts of gifts. One man gets five, another two, a third gets one. In this detail I think Jesus is simply reflecting life as we experience it. Some people are gifted in ways that will be visible and celebrated in this world; others are gifted in ways that remain quiet and unseen.

The variable that does matter is what each servant does with what he's been given. Here there are three servants because Jesus wants to make it painstakingly clear that the size of the gift is not the crucial variable. Even though the first servant receives a gift much larger than the second, the master responds in identical fashion to each of them. Jesus wants us to understand that the visible level of giftedness and calling is not the hinge point. Whether I'm a five-talent, two-talent, or one-talent person is not what counts in the long run.

I must ruthlessly refuse to compare my talents with anyone else.

Comparison will lead to pride and a false sense of superiority if I'm ahead of someone, and misery if I'm behind. Or worse, I will discount and bury the irreplaceable treasure that the Lord of the Gift has given to me alone.

Have you been comparing what you've been given with someone else—physical appearance, intelligence, relationships, accomplishments, energy level, or temperament?

I must come to identify, cultivate, invest, prize, and enjoy the gifts that have been given to me. The Lord of the Gift is very wise. He knew exactly what he was doing when he created you. He is well-pleased that you exist. He has entrusted to you everything you need to fulfill the purpose for which you were created.

At the end of the day, God will not ask you why you didn't lead someone else's life or invest someone else's gifts. He will not ask, *What did you do with what you didn't have?*

Though, he will ask, *What did you do with what you had?*

Comparison is not an adequate excuse for the tragedy of an unopened gift.

> The Lord of the Gift is very wise. He knew exactly what he was doing when he created you.

When the lord of the settled account came to the third servant, he gave another rationale for his passivity: "For I knew that you were a hard man, reaping where you do not sow, and I was *afraid,* so I hid what you gave me." He wanted a promise that nothing would go wrong, not a command to do what's right.

Fear makes people bury the treasure God has given them.

Fear makes people disobedient to the calling of the master.

Recently a friend asked me a question about an area in my life for which the true answer would have been embarrassing, and I didn't want to be embarrassed. So I just lied.

I had to go back and do repair work that was very painful for me. When I look back on it, I wonder, *Why did I lie?*

Why do I ever lie? Usually to avoid pain. I am afraid of what will happen if I tell the truth. Fear prompts me to lie. And it's not just deceit.

When people are gossiping, I join in even though I know it's wrong because I am afraid of being left out.

I hoard possessions because I am afraid I'll be bored or insecure if I don't have a lot of stuff.

I flatter someone because I am afraid he or she won't like me if I don't.

Fear of being poor is what made Jacob deceive his father.

Fear made the Israelites in the wilderness slight God's calling and care and clamor to return to Egypt.

Fear of having to suffer is what made the disciples run away from Jesus.

And what made Peter deny Jesus three times?

Fear made these disciples betray their deepest value to their best friend at his hour of greatest need.

Look at most sin—yours and mine—and underneath it you will find fear.

I am afraid that if I risk obeying God, he will not take care of me. I will not be all right and something will happen that I cannot handle.

In Scripture, when God calls Moses, Joshua, Gideon, or Esther to do something great for him, the single greatest obstacle that stands in the way is *fear*.

But we find a major surprise here. When the servant says fear of the master inhibited him, the master doesn't contradict him. The master does not say, *You have misunderstood me! Whether you use your gift or waste it doesn't really matter to me. I see this is painful for you, and my primary goal for you is to spare you pain—I'm so sorry I brought it up. Let's bury the whole issue.*

The master graciously lets pass the slur on his character. He doesn't remind the servant how generous he was in first place—that he had given this servant the chance of a lifetime. He says,

You got this much right: it matters to me. Your life—what you do with what I gave you—is a matter of supreme importance.

If that's really what you thought, at least you should have done something. You could have invested the money and gotten interest.

Jesus is pointing out that this rationale is just a smoke screen and not a serious reason for his action. This guy is simply trying to finesse his way out of a ticket. But that will not happen, because the master is the lord of the settled account; he cannot be finessed.

Fear is not an adequate excuse for the tragedy of an unopened gift.

One of the most sobering aspects of the story is that the servant is judged, not for doing *bad* things, but for doing *nothing*. He didn't steal or embezzle or defraud. He merely buried his gift.

Jesus uses two very serious words to describe him: wicked and lazy. We don't use these two words together much anymore. Nowadays hardly anyone would admit to laziness.

When someone is asked in a job interview about personal weaknesses, what is inevitably the answer? *I push myself too hard. My standards are too high. I expect too much of myself—work, work, work.* When is last time you heard someone say, *My problem is that I'm just too lazy. I can sit on the sofa, eat bonbons, and watch game shows by the month.*

But historically, sloth was taken so seriously by Christians that it was listed as one of the Seven Deadly Sins. In fact, Solomon Schimmel points out that it is a specifically spiritual sin—the only one of the seven not included in Greco-Roman lists of vices. This is because the Judeo-Christian tradition understood human beings as responsible to God. Therefore our lives are not about self-preservation and fulfillment, but are to be acts of stewardship. To fail to be good stewards of what God has given us is a form of robbing him.

> Our lives are not about self-preservation and fulfillment, but are to be acts of stewardship.

Sloth as a spiritual sin is not the same thing as physical laziness. It can co-exist with much busyness. It is the failure to do what needs to be done when it needs doing—like the kamikaze pilot who flew seventeen missions. At its core, sloth consists of "loss of meaning, purpose, and hope, coupled with indifference to the welfare of others." It is the opposite of zeal and joy in the service of God.

This aspect of the story—that Jesus came down so hard on the third servant simply for *inactivity*—has always troubled some people. In a second-century manuscript, *The Gospel of the Nazarene*, the story was repeated, but the writer added a phrase to describe the third servant: "He squandered all his money on harlots and flute players." Evidently the writer felt that simply "doing nothing" was not enough to warrant Jesus' harsh words, so he added embezzlement and immorality to the servant's sin—he blew the bank account on prostitutes and flautists. (Apparently those were the two worst categories of people the writer could think of. I'm not sure why flute players got such a bad rap.) But there were no harlots or flute players in Jesus' story. They weren't needed.

Max DePree writes that unrealized potential is a sin—a very serious sin. This is a story about the sin of unrealized potential—the tragedy of the unopened gift. This is why one of the great temptations most of us face that could block us from getting out of the boat is comfort. Comfort will often keep us from growth.

Fifty years ago, we began to orient our lives around one of the great growth-avoidance inventions of all time: TV. You didn't have to think, focus your attention, or follow a closely reasoned chain of thought when you were watching *Leave It to Beaver*. But even then you had to get up out of your chair, walk all the way to the set, laboriously change the channel *by hand*—which was exhausting, so we invented the ... remote control. Now mankind could change channels from the La-Z-Boy, as God intended.

You want to see how devoted we are to comfort? Walk into the average American home and hide the remote control, and watch what happens. Life without the remote control is an unbearable burden for the average American family. Then someone invented a TV with a beeper so that when you clap your hands, the remote control will beep until you find it.

What's most depressing about all this is that I know some people will read this chapter and the only thing they will take away from it is, *I gotta get one of those TVs with a beeper for the remote.*

But too much comfort is dangerous. Literally. Researchers at the University of California at Berkeley did an experiment sometime ago that involved introducing an amoeba into a perfectly stress-free environment. Ideal temperature, optimal concentration of moisture, constant food supply—the amoeba had an environment to which it had to make no adjustment whatsoever. So you would guess that that was one happy little amoeba. Whatever it is that gives amoebas ulcers and high blood pressure was gone.

Yet, oddly enough, it died.

Apparently there is something about all living creatures, even amoebas, that demands challenge. We require change, adaptation, and challenge the way we require food and air. Comfort alone will kill us.

When teachers want students to grow, they don't give them answers—they give them problems! (*"If a train leaves Cleveland at 3:00 going 50 m.p.h. . . . ."*) It is only in the process of accepting and solving problems that our ability to think creatively is enhanced, our persistence is strengthened, and our self-confidence is deepened. If someone gives me the answers, I may get a good score on a test, but I will not have grown. Just as our bodies simply will not grow stronger without being challenged to the point of exertion, so it is with our mind and spirit.

Comfort is not an adequate excuse for an unopened gift.

Which Way Are You Following?

I want to ask you to exercise your imagination for a moment. Imagine that your life is over, and you are led to a small room. There are two chairs in the room, one for you and one for God (who gets a very large chair), and there's a VCR. God puts a tape into the machine. It has your name on it and is labeled *What Might Have Been.*

> Imagine watching all that God might have done with your life if you had let him.

Imagine watching all that God might have done with your life if you had let him.

47

Imagine seeing what he might have done with your financial resources if you had trusted him to be generous. Imagine seeing what he might have done with your giftedness if you had trusted him enough to be daring. Imagine what he might have done in your relationships if you had trusted him enough to be fully truthful and fully loving. Imagine what he might have done with your character, if you had dared to confess sin, acknowledge temptation, and pursue growth.

I don't know that God will make any of us watch a video like that. I do know that if I think too much about how far I fall short of what might have been, it can become defeating and that unrealized potential can become a club I beat myself over the head with.

But I also know that I want my life to come as close as I can to realizing the goodness God intended for it. I know this is my only chance, and I know I want to minimize the gap between what shall be and what might have been as much as I can. I know that as long as I'm living, it's not too late—because I have this day. I know I want to ask God for commands, not guarantees, because when God commands, he enables. (St. Jerome said about Jesus' response to Peter, "You command, and immediately waters are solids.") And I know that one day it will have been worth it.

He Is the Lord of the Reward

There is one last truth about the master Jesus wants us to understand. The Lord of the Gift and the Lord of the Settled Account is also the Lord of the Reward. He has wonderful things in store for those who steward his treasure wisely.

Some aspects of what the master says are pretty much what we would expect: *Well done, good and faithful servant.* Imagine receiving this commendation from God! He also invites the servant to enter into the master's happiness. This is some serious joy.

But there is a surprise here as well. The master doesn't say, *Now you can float on lovely fluffy clouds, and live in a very nice condo with lots of upgrades, and sing in the choir that will sing the same songs for a hundred billion years.*

Instead he says, "You have been trustworthy in *a few things*. Now I will put you in charge of *many things*."

Now it is time for you to get on with your real work! Remember, the master had given the servant an enormous amount of wealth. Yet he says, "You have been trustworthy in *a few things.*" Can this be true—that greater wealth than any of them had seen or imagined amounts to *a few things?* Yes—compared with what's coming. Compared with what's in store for his servants, the wealth of the Sultan of Brunei, the power of Napoleon, and the fame of Michael Jordan constitute "a few things."

When I was in grade school, I sang in a church choir directed by a woman named Sigrid. She had blue hair, a wide vibrato, and several chins, all of which threatened to go off when she directed with vigor. When she got frustrated with us (which we often gave her good reason to be), she would clap her hands and say, "Children, start singing like I told you—because when you get to heaven, it's all you're going to do: sing, sing, sing, morning, noon, night—so you'd better get it right."

Somehow the idea of five to ten billion years in choir robes under the direction of Sigrid and those chins didn't sound like eternal bliss.

Many people have vague ideas about floating around in eternal cloud banks. They picture heaven as an eternal retirement village. I had a friend who used to ask me, "Will there be golf in heaven?" His reasoning went like this:

> Heaven will be what makes me happy—it takes golf to make me happy—therefore there will be golf in heaven.

I had to explain that while there will be joy in heaven, I might have to grow to become the kind of person who experiences joy in God's community. Besides, the Bible says that in heaven there will be no lying, no cheating, no "weeping and wailing and gnashing of teeth"—so how could there be golf? There will be no golf in heaven. Tennis, yes, but no golf.

From this story of the talents we learn that heaven will be nothing at all like an eternal retirement village. In fact, heaven will be that place where we finally experience the fullness of adventure, creativity, and fruitfulness we were made for.

Jesus said, "To the one who conquers I will give a place with me on my throne, just as I myself conquered and sat down with my Father on his throne."

You can be sure that that throne is not a La-Z-Boy. Part of the reward of heaven is that we will finally see the full potential of humanity realized—including ours. Heaven will be the ultimate place of *realized potential*. There will be no unopened gifts there.

So why don't you take a moment to ask some questions:

—What is my deepest dream?
—How much passion do I experience in my daily life?
—What do I want my epitaph to say?
—How much am I growing these days?
—How often do I take risks that require a power greater than my own?
—If I had to name the "one true thing" that I believe I was set on this earth to do, what would it be?
—How clear is it to me?

What has the Lord of the Gift given to you that you need to invest in the kingdom? Maybe it's your mind. Your mind can be a place of unrealized potential, saturated with whatever is on billboards or in the mass media. You can fill it with junk, jealousy, greed, anger, or fear.

Or, your mind can be renewed. Filled with thoughts that are good, noble, true, and courageous. But you will have to invest it. Maybe it's your material possessions. Your bank account can be a place of unrealized potential. You can use money to accumulate stuff. Or, your money can build the church, spread the gospel, feed the poor, develop cities.

John Wesley wrote that Christians have just three rules to follow regarding material possessions:

Make all you can—save all you can—give all you can.

A friend of mine wrote that apparently American evangelicals have decided that two out of three ain't bad.

You could make a secret, sacrificial gift this week—that's an eternal investment. Maybe it's your time and your talent.

You can drift: get up, go to work, come home, eat supper, watch TV, retire, and die.

Or, you can take each moment and say, "God, this is yours." You can offer him your spiritual giftedness—not compared with anyone else—as fully honed and developed as you can get it, identified with pristine clarity, cultivated with relentless perseverance, deployed with unstoppable vigor, submitted with sacrificial humility, and celebrated with raucous joy.

You may have lavish talents,—resources of finances or networks or abilities that could produce huge returns for the Lord of the Gift— and you're just sitting on them. They're buried. It's time for you to get in the game. I tell you without apology investing all you have in the kingdom of God is the greatest opportunity you will ever know.

You may feel that, from a human perspective, what you have to offer doesn't count for much, that it will never be very visible or dramatic.

Jesus has made it clear: There is no truth in such a perspective. We serve the Lord of the Gift.

The Lord of the Gift can take five fish and two loaves and feed the multitudes. The Lord of the Gift can take two mites given by an impoverished widow and make it the lead gift in the whole campaign. The Lord of the Gift can take a stuttering fugitive named Moses and defy a world-power dictator and his army. The Lord of the Gift can go from a bloodstained cross to an empty tomb. The Lord of the Gift can take twelve bumbling followers and create a community that has spread throughout the world with a dream that refuses to die.

> He can take what you have to offer and make a difference that matters for eternity.

He is a surprisingly resourceful person, the Lord of the Gift. He can take what you have to offer and make a difference that matters for eternity.

You have no idea what your potential is. For there is no reward like the reward of the opened gift.

"Beloved, we are God's children now; what we will be has not yet been revealed."

But it will be revealed when the Lord of the Gift returns.

GETTING OUT OF THE BOAT

1. Think back to the story of the china and the box. What is the greatest gift God has given to you—what's in your box?
2. In what area of life (vocational, relational, or intellectual, for instance) are you experiencing the most growth these days?
3. Where are you most in danger of becoming a boat potato?
4. This chapter lists three reasons why people bury their treasure: comparison, fear, and sloth. Which of these (or what other factor) could most tempt you to miss your "chance of a lifetime"? Why?
5. Take some time to imagine the scene where you and God review your life together. What single step could you take today to most minimize the regret factor at the end of your life?

Peter answered him, "Lord, if it is you, command me to come to you on the water." He said, "Come."

Matthew 14:28–29

Discerning the Call

Living means being addressed.

Martin Buber

Water-walking requires not only the courage to take a risk, but also the wisdom to discern a call.

A man appears before the pearly gates.

"Have you ever done anything of particular merit?" St. Peter asks.

"Well, I can think of one thing," the man offers. "Once I came upon a gang of high-testosterone bikers who were threatening a young woman. I directed them to leave her alone, but they wouldn't listen. So I approached the largest and most heavily tattooed biker. I smacked him on the head, kicked his bike over, ripped out his nose ring and threw it on the ground, and told him, 'Leave her alone now or you'll answer to me.'"

St. Peter was impressed. "When did this happen?"

"A couple of minutes ago."

There is a big difference between faith and foolishness. Historically, commentators have differed on whether Peter's desire to leave the boat was an expression of devotion or an impulse control problem. Calvin said it was given as a warning against "over-much rashness" and foolish risk taking. On the other hand, Chrysostom viewed this as an act of a disciple's love; he noted that Peter did not say in pride, "Bid me walk on the water," but in devotion, "Bid me come unto thee."

Whichever way you view it, one of the striking aspects of the story as Matthew tells it is that Peter does not immediately jump out of the boat. He begins by requesting Jesus to give him permission first. ("Lord, if it is you, command me to come to you on the water.")

Why does Peter do this? After all, he certainly does not have a problem acting out his impulses:

On the Mount of Transfiguration, Peter suggested that they stay there and build altars to Jesus, Moses, and Elijah. We are told Peter blurted out this idea "because he did not know what to say." Many people, when they do not know what to say, simply refrain from saying anything, preferring to wait until they have more information. Not Peter.

In the garden of Gethsemane, surrounded by Roman soldiers, Peter impulsively grabbed a sword and lopped off the ear of a soldier named Malchus. Jesus had to reach down, grab the ear, and superglue it back to Malchus's head. We can only imagine Jesus' words: *I apologize for my associate here. I have been working with him for years—I still can't do much with him.*

At Caesarea Philippi, when Jesus predicted his coming death, Peter advised him to soft-pedal the cross talk on the grounds that it was bad for morale. Jesus' initial response—"Get thee behind me, Satan"—could not have enhanced Peter's reputation for giving wise advice.

Matthew's portrait of Peter makes it quite clear that he was in touch with his inner impulsive child. So why does he pause here to ask for a command first before climbing out of the boat?

I believe that Matthew wants his readers to understand a crucial aspect about water-walking: Peter is not in charge of water-walking—Jesus is. This is not some power at Peter's disposal to use anytime he chooses, for whatever purpose he pleases. Before he gets out of the boat, he had better make sure that this is what he is called to do and that Jesus is the one doing the calling. Jesus is looking for something more than mere impulsiveness. Sometimes people make reckless decisions—about relationships, finances, or work—and then rationalize it with a veneer of spiritual language. So it is worth considering for a moment what water-walking is not.

Psychologist Frank Farley has spent thirty years researching what he calls the Type T, or thrill-seeking personality. These are people who are drawn to high-risk situations and behaviors. They prefer uncertainty, unpredictability, high novelty, and much variety. They are easily bored and crave constant stimulation.

Israeli scientists have actually identified what is being called the risk-taking gene. People identified as excitable and curious had a longer version of a gene known as D4DR than reflective and laid-back subjects. Type Ts engage in what have come to be known as "extreme sports": mountain climbing, parasailing, hang gliding, and BASE jumping. The last consists of leaping off a cliff or a bridge and praying your chute opens up in the few seconds it takes you to fall three thousand feet. It is both illegal and highly dangerous. Forty-six BASE jumpers have died during its short history of eighteen years.

It is interesting to note that in most self-help books, risk-taking is highly praised. But in literature on psychological research, it is mostly a danger sign. High Type Ts, although they can do great things, are also more prone toward potentially destructive behavior like substance abuse, high-risk sexual activity, and compulsive gambling.

Sometimes—especially when life feels boring or unfulfilling, or I sense it is passing me by—I can impatiently demand that all my problems be solved at once by making a rash decision that is not in line with God's call for my life. It is possible for us to make courageous, high-risk decisions that are stupid.

Garrison Keillor writes about Pastor Ingqvist, who was occasionally alarmed when he glanced at the "Dear Abby" column and noticed how often she referred her writers to ministers:

> "Talk to your minister" she'd say to the fourteen-year-old girl in love with the fifty-one-year-old auto mechanic (married) who is in prison for rape. Why did Abby assume that a minister could deal with this?...
>
> Poor man. Things were fairly clear to him a moment before, and now, as she pours out her love for Vince, her belief in his innocence, the fact that his wife never loved him, never really loved him, not like she, Trish, can love him, and the fact that despite his age and their never having met except in letters, there

is something indescribably sacred and precious between them, all the pastor can think is "You're crazy. Don't be ridiculous!" **Thou shalt not be ridiculous.** Paul says, 'See then that ye walk circumspectly, not as fools, but as wise, redeeming the time, because the days are evil.' How does this apply specifically to Trish, in love by mail …? When Paul wrote that wonderful sentence, he probably was sitting in an upper room in Athens; it was late at night, quiet, and all the fools were asleep. He could write the simple truth, and no fool was around to say, "Huh? What do you mean? Are you saying I shouldn't go for the world long-distance walking-backward record? But I know I can do it! I'm good at it! I can walk backward for miles."

The line between "Thou shalt not be afraid" and "Thou shalt not be ridiculous" is often a fine one and not easily located. Knowing when to get out of the boat and take a risk does not only demand courage; it also demands the wisdom to ask the right questions, the discernment to recognize the voice of the Master, and the patience to wait for his command.

Jesus is not looking for impulse-ridden Type Ts. He is looking for what might be called the Type W, or water-walking personality. This involves the desire for adventure with God—the God-gene—and we all have one. It is part of our spiritual DNA. It requires both courage to take risks and wisdom to know which risks to take.

So how do I discern the difference between an authentic call from God to get out of the boat from my own rash impulse? How do I become a Type W follower? To probe this question further, let us consider the biblical notion of calling.

Calling: A Reflection of God's Image

We begin with a theological question: What does God do all day?

If you had to answer that question in a single word, what would you say? For most of us, if we are on an extended vacation or for some reason have a large block of unfilled time, *What will I do today?* is a major question. *I'm bored* is the primary complaint of both childhood and retirement. We are talking about the need to "kill some time" in such situations. God has all eternity. What does he do with all that time? Think he mostly sits around watching stuff?

The biblical writers tell us what God does in a single phrase: He works.

Leland Ryken notes that Christianity is quite unique in this regard. The ancient Greeks, for instance, viewed the gods as being above work. Mount Olympus was a kind of divine Palm Springs where, aside from hurling the occasional thunderbolt, Zeus and his associates lived in Leisure World. In contrast, the opening lines of Genesis are filled with God's work—he separates light from darkness, makes the sky and heavenly bodies, gathers the waters, forms human beings from dust.

And after the sixth day, God does not go into retirement. The psalmist is quite clear that the universe does not run by mechanical necessity; it is run by God.

> You make springs gush forth in the valleys;...
> From your lofty abode you water the mountains;
>   the earth is satisfied with the fruit of your work.
> You cause the grass to grow for the cattle,
>   and plants for people to use....
> O LORD, how manifold are your works!

God is particularly active in working with people. The psalmist says that the God of Israel will "neither slumber nor sleep," but is always guiding and protecting his flock.

When Jesus came to earth, he came as a worker. In fact, for most of his adult life he worked as a carpenter. (People in our day pay a fortune for a Chippendale chair—imagine having a bench made by Jesus!) Jesus leaves no doubt that he works, for he says, "My Father is still working, and I also am working."

God is described in the Bible by many metaphors that involve work: He is a gardener, an artist, a potter, a shepherd, a king, a homemaker, and a builder.

"The God of the Bible," writes Paul Minear, "is pre-eminently a worker." He is highly interested in, understands the joy of, and is deeply committed to work. This is significant because at the climax of the creation story we are told "the LORD God formed man from the dust of the ground, and breathed into his nostrils the breath of life; and the man became a living being."

You are a piece of work by God! If you have ever had someone, maybe a boss or a spouse, say sarcastically to you, *"You're a piece of work,"* it is literally true. And because you were made in God's image, you were also created to do work. You were made to create, lead, study, organize, heal, cultivate, or teach. Arthur Miller writes that this is what lies at the heart of seven-days-a-week faith: *"It is using one's endowed giftedness to serve the world with excellence and, through that service, to love and honor God!* The calling that fully engages what God has given you is a holy task!"

> **You are a piece of work by God.**

You have a calling, but callings are not always easy to hear. Like young Samuel, we may not always recognize whose voice it is that asks us to do something. Gregg Levoy notes that in Scripture, God often calls to the prophets by repeating their names twice: "Abraham, Abraham. Jacob, Jacob. Moses, Moses." Once is not always enough.

So how do ordinary human beings go about discovering their callings?

Taking your Calling Seriously

When my children were young and we bought them gifts, the three words I dreaded most were *Some assembly required.* I don't do assembly. Not well, anyway. Inevitably there would be numerous parts left over, laying sadly alone and disconnected on the carpet. I always felt bad for these parts. They had no role to play, no chance to make the team. I always figured someone at the factory slipped up and put useless parts in the package—spare parts.

This is not how God works. He does not make spare parts. *You* are not a spare part. You have a purpose—a design that is central to God's dream for the human race. We are, first of all, according to Scripture, called to know God, to receive his love and mercy, and to be his children. We are called to live in the reality of his kingdom and to have Christ formed in us.

As a crucial part of your calling, you were given certain gifts, talents, longings, and desires. To identify these with clarity, to develop them with skill, and to use them joyfully and humbly to serve God and his creation is central to why you were created.

John Belushi and Dan Ackroyd once starred in a movie called *The Blues Brothers*. They played a couple of ex-convict-wanna-be musicians who were trying to raise money for an orphanage. Anytime they were asked about their work, they had a standard response: "We're on a mission from God." They always said it as if they believed it. The very idea that two inept, unworthy human beings could be on a mission from God was, of course, the central joke of the whole story.

Here is the story of your life: You are on a mission from God.

Either that is true, or you have no purpose, no mission at all. Jesus put it like this: *You are the salt of the earth. You are the light of the world.* Others have come before you. Others will come after you. But this is your day. If God's kingdom is to manifest itself right now, it will have to be through you. God himself will not come to take your place. *You are on a mission from God.*

The place to begin is by taking your calling with the right kind of seriousness. There is an old Hasidic story in which everyone is commanded to wear a coat with two pockets to receive messages from God. In one pocket is written: *You are nothing but one of millions upon millions of grains of sand in the universe.* In the other pocket it says: *I made the universe just for you.*

I can wear my calling lightly. I can live free of the fear of failure, without being preoccupied by how my career looks to others, knowing my salvation and worth as a person are not at stake in my job title.

But what we do matters immensely. It is worth devoting our best energy to. *We are on a mission from God.*

Honoring Your Raw Material

In addition to taking it seriously, discerning a calling requires one of the greatest challenges of self-exploration and judgment a human being can undertake. Callings are usually not easy to discover. You will have to be ruthlessly honest about your gifts and your limitations. You will have to be willing to ask hard questions and live with the answers. Discerning God's calling will take many attempts and failures. You will have to be willing to let some dreams die a painful death. You did not arrive on this planet with your calling pre-clarified and your gifts pre-developed. You arrived with a little warning: *Some assembly required.*

A calling is something you discover, not something you choose. The word *vocation* comes from the Latin word for voice. Discovering it involves very careful listening. People will sometimes speak about "choosing their calling," but a chosen calling is an oxymoron. The whole idea of a calling is taken from Scripture, where time after time God calls someone to do his work. The whole idea of calling is that there is a Call-er and a call-ee.

You and I are the call-ees and God is the Call-er. God equips the worker and assigns the work. Michael Novak puts it like this:

> We didn't give ourselves the personalities, talents, or longings we were born with. When we fulfill these—these gifts from beyond ourselves—it is like fulfilling something we were meant to do.... the Creator of all things knows the name of each of us—knows thoroughly, better than we do ourselves, what is in us, for he put it there and intends for us to do something with it—something that meshes with his intentions for many other people.... Even if we do not always think of it that way, each of us was given a calling—by fate, by chance, by destiny, by God. Those who are lucky have found it.

Parker Palmer, a Quaker educator and writer, offers an added thought: "Everything in the universe has a nature, which means limits as well as potential." One of the competencies of artistry and craftsmanship is knowing how to discern the nature of the material you are working with. Great sculptors spend much time studying a piece of marble before they ever take a chisel to it; they describe what they do not so much as imposing a shape on the marble as in releasing what it has always contained. Skilled potters know that as they knead and press clay, it presses back, telling them what it can and cannot become. Amateurs lack this discernment—when I was in seventh grade, every lump of clay was a potential ashtray.

A calling is something you discover, not something you choose.

You also have a nature with your own potential and limits. Frederich Buechner wrote that calling is "the place where your deep gladness meets the world's deep need." It is not hard to figure out where the world's deep need is. It is everywhere! What turns out to be more difficult than you might expect is discovering where your deep gladness lies. What work brings you joy? For what do you have desire and passion—for these, too, are gifts from God. This is why giftedness is about more than just talents—it includes *passion*. As Arthur Miller says, "It's the lifeblood of a person, the song that her heart longs to sing, the race that his legs were born to run.... There's an electricity associated with giftedness. Give a person the chance, and he'll jolt you."

One of my favorite pictures of the "deep gladness" that God intends for his creation is in Psalm 19, where the psalmist says, "In the heavens he has set a tent for the sun, which comes out like a bridegroom from his wedding canopy, and like a strong man runs its course with joy."

I love to think of the strong man—*a champion*, some translations put it—exulting in the race. He knows he's going to be taxed and stretched; he knows it will take everything he's got. But he loves the race. He relishes the challenge. He competes, not for the trophy at the end, but for the love of the game.

This is the teacher facing a room full of skeptical students with the challenge of opening the door of learning to them.

This is the leader who looks at an organization with morale challenges and resource limitations and can't wait to sound the trumpet and unleash people's potential.

This is the writer resenting a blank screen and hating the deadline, but knowing there is no other joy than that of creating.

This is the gardener who loves to create beauty; the accountant who finds joy in order; the nurse who delights in healing; the mechanic who takes pride in the skill of clever hands.

That does not mean that following a calling always brings feelings of enjoyment. Often it means the gritty resolution to bear with a hard task when it would be easier to quit. But even this yields a certain satisfaction when I know I have been skilled and fitted by God for the task. But I must be ruthlessly honest about *my* deep gladness.

Parker Palmer's wonderful book *Let Your Life Speak* has much to say about discovering one's vocation. He writes about the time when, because of his growing prominence in educational circles, he was offered the presidency of an educational institution. It would have meant an increase in pay, status, and influence—from a career standpoint, it was a no-brainer.

But the Quakers have a tradition where, when faced with an important decision about calling, they gather a half-dozen friends to serve as a "clearness committee." This committee gathers primarily to ask questions so as to discern God's calling more clearly. (Palmer confesses, however, that in his case, "Looking back ... it is clear that my real intent in convening this group was not to discern anything but to brag about being offered a job I had already decided to accept!")

For a while the questions were easy—what would Parker's vision be for this school; what mission would it serve in society, and so on. Then someone asked what appeared to be a very simple question: "Parker, what would you like about being president?"

Oddly enough, Parker had to think about this one for a while. "Well, I wouldn't like all the politics involved; I wouldn't like having to give up my study and teaching; I wouldn't like to have to raise funds...."

"Yes," the questioner reminded him, "but the question was what *would* you like?"

"I'm coming to that," he said irritably, then proceeded to list several more irksome things. "I wouldn't like to have to give up my summer vacations, I wouldn't like..."

The question was called for a third time. Palmer writes,

> I felt compelled to give the only honest answer I possessed, an answer that came from the very bottom of my barrel, an answer that appalled even me as I spoke it. "Well," said I, in the smallest voice I possess, "I guess what I'd like most is getting my picture in the paper with the word president under it." I was sitting with seasoned Quakers who knew that though my answer was laughable, my mortal soul was clearly at stake! They did not laugh at all but went into a long and serious silence—a silence in which I could only sweat and inwardly groan.

Finally my questioner broke the silence with a question that cracked all of us up—and cracked me open: "Parker" he said, "can you think of an easier way to get your picture in the paper?"

If Palmer had taken the job, think of what the results would have been in his life: fatigue, discouragement, a loss of joy, lack of energy, and a sense of inadequacy. This is one of the causes of what psychologists have come to call the "imposter phenomenon"—the sense that people (especially successful people) often have of spending too much time and effort trying to conceal their inadequacy from others. If he were like most of us, Palmer then would have been tempted to think that the problem was that he had joined a dysfunctional organization, or that the board had let him down, or that he had a troublesome faculty.

"You cannot choose your calling," Palmer says. "You must let your life speak." By this phrase he means that an enormous part of following our calling is not so much choosing as it is *listening*. From early on, you have been drawn to certain activities, certain ways of being and doing. These ways may not be applauded by your family or your company. You may prize solitude in the midst of a culture that rewards extroversion. You may crave spontaneity in a subculture that praises predictability. It will take care and courage to discover and to be true to the person God made you to be. Over time, your heart will seek to make its longings known.

> Our calling is not so much choosing as it is *listening*.

Perhaps you were created to learn and, by your learning, to benefit others. You will find yourself drawn to reading, reflecting, writing, and teaching. But if you are convinced that you must be a corporate success for your life to count, you will saw against the grain of your life. You will refuse to let your life speak.

Maybe you are a woman who loves to lead teams, to sound trumpets and charge up hills. But if you have been told that women are not to do such things, that you must stay in the background, you will bury the gift you were given. You will refuse to let your life speak.

It is very important to distinguish what I love doing for its own sake from what I may want to do because of the rewards it may bring me.

Researcher Mihaly Csikszentmihalyi did a study involving two hundred artists eighteen years after they left art school. He found it was those who in their student days savored the sheer joy of painting that became serious painters. Those drawn to art school in hopes of wealth or fame drifted away to other professions. "Painters must want to paint above all else. If the artist in front of the canvas begins to wonder how much he will sell it for, or what the critics will think of it, he won't be able to pursue original avenues. Creative achievements depend on single-minded immersion."

Sometimes this choice—the decision to let one's life speak—has spelled the difference between failure and greatness. William McFeely's biography of Ulysses Grant describes a man who was masterfully fitted for military leadership and writing (his *Memoirs* are considered a classic of military literature) but horribly ill-equipped for business and politics. Grant neither understood nor enjoyed life in Washington, and he is usually judged to have been one of the least effective presidents of the United States. In his final—and extraordinary—State of the Union message, he apologized for his ineptness: "It was my fortune, or misfortune, to be called to the office of Chief Executive without any previous political training."

Why, then, did this Civil War hero work so hard for a job he neither enjoyed nor understood? "His personal need was to retain the immense respect in which he was held everywhere in the North.... He wanted to matter in a world he had been watching closely all his life. A little recognition—a little understanding that he did know what he was doing—was all he required. He needed to be taken into account." His own unmet needs for acceptance and wholeness blinded him to acknowledging his limitations. He did not truly love the job—it is as if he merely desired his picture in the paper with the word *president* under it.

All of us face this challenge. A man I know, whose father was very successful, decided he had to go into that same line of work. He was not pressured into it, and indeed, he might have resisted such a career if he faced that pressure. This snare was much more subtle. In part, it was that his dad's success opened doors for him in this field that might have been closed in other arenas; in part, it was because when he was growing up, this was the field in which accomplishment was always discussed and celebrated. At any rate, he has spent twenty years now trying to be his dad, trying to convince himself that he is doing pretty well at it; yet, as he moves through his work, that argument is getting harder and harder to maintain. Reality—*I am not my father; I don't have the same kind of gifts and drives he has*—would be too painful for him. His wife sees this more clearly and tries to tell him sometimes, but he cannot hear her. He does not honor his raw material.

I can think of a woman who craves attention and is certain that she must succeed as an actress or singer so she can get it. She clings to this dream even in the face of overwhelming evidence that it does not reflect whom God made her to be. She clings to it so tightly that whenever anyone tries to tell her she may be making a mistake, it causes her unbearable pain. She feels they are rejecting her, so she runs away. She does not honor her raw material.

When I do not honor my raw material, reality becomes my enemy. I close my eyes and ears to all the indications that I am trying to pursue what I am not called or gifted to do. But underneath I am condemned to live in chronic, low-grade anxiety that whispers to me that I am trying to be someone I'm not.

If I have the courage to acknowledge my limits and embrace them, I can experience enormous freedom. If I lack this courage, I will be imprisoned by them. Some of my limitations do not bother me much. It does not really concern me that I am unable to operate power tools or draw a straight line. But I have a few limitations that are exceedingly painful to me. They involve dreams that I have carried with me for as long as I can remember. Acknowledging those limitations has felt a lot like dying to me. It has sometimes left me wondering whether I have a true calling at all.

I think of people I know who possess tremendous minds. They have a depth of learning and insight that enables them to make lasting contributions to the search for truth and knowledge. They sit at the table of what philosopher Mortimer Adler calls the "Great Conversation" of the human race. I was bright enough to do well in school and reach a certain level of learning, but I will never have a mind like that. I will not sit at the table.

I watch leaders who have enormous energy to lead, who carry deep within them reserves of optimism and confidence to fuel those under them, who have a kind of inner gyroscope that guides them to develop others and achieve a mission. I admire these gifts highly and have often found myself pained or confused in trying to do an honest self-assessment of them.

Parker Palmer writes about the myth of the limitless self:

> Like many middle-class Americans, especially those who are white and male, I was raised in a subculture that insisted I could do anything I wanted to, be anything I wanted to be, if I were willing to make the effort. The message was that both the universe and I were without limits, given enough energy and commitment on my part. God made things that way, and all I had to do was to get with the program.
>
> My troubles began, of course, when I started to slam into my limitations, especially in the form of failure.

Even as I write these words, I recall failures that are the most disappointing to me. Many years after they occur, the memory of my failures still holds the power to make me want to forget them, hide from them, or explain them away. The reason for some of these failures was not simply a lack of persistence or unfriendly circumstances (which might just call for more effort); I was slamming into my own limitations. It is a humbling thing for me to realize how often in my life my own need to be seen as a successful, strong, confident, charismatic leader has caused me to run from patiently examining my failures and learning from them who I am and who I am not.

I think of the dreams I had for a church I helped plant that did not grow into what those of us at the core hoped and prayed it might become. I know that, as least in part, my limitations played a role. One of the great challenges of life is learning from an experience like that both with truth that enables me to live in reality *and* grace that reminds me that I have a calling from God and adequate gifts to fulfill it. I am convinced that if I face up to acknowledging the limitations that pain me most, there is enormous freedom and joy on the other side.

I believe that each of us has similar experiences, which is why I think some of the most important, yet difficult questions for a person to ask are *What is your most painful limitation? What is the limitation that frightens you most to acknowledge and accept? Where do you most avoid seeing the deep truth about yourself?*

Assemble Your Own "Clearness Committee"

Likewise, one of the hardest commands in Scripture to obey is Paul's statement to regard yourself with "sober judgment." To come to an accurate assessment of my passions, gifts, and limits is one of the great challenges of life. In part, this command requires tremendous self-awareness. But I am also likely to need some help from other people to overcome my blind spots.

When I think of the value of receiving discernment from more than one person, from a "clearness committee," I think of Bob Buford. Bob was an immensely successful television tycoon who sensed God was calling him to get out of a very well-appointed boat. In the words of his book *Halftime,* he wanted to move from "success to significance." He and his wife, Linda, met at length with one adviser, who helped him clarify his sense of purpose immensely. Then this adviser suggested a questionable next step: "Sell your company and invest in the ministry-oriented projects you've been talking about." Bob writes,

> I sat there, stunned by the implications of this decision. Linda appeared no less stunned. I could almost see the stereotypical images of ministers, missionaries, and monastics passing through her mind. Would we be a philanthropic couple passing out money until our sack was empty? Would we be required to dress like a minister and his spouse?

Bob goes on to explain how he assembled his own clearness committee (though he didn't use that language). Together they helped him see that what he loves most and does best involves strategic thinking and organizational leadership. They discerned that if he were to sell his company, he would lose a platform that could be leveraged for a great deal of good. Instead, they helped him see that his passions and competencies were ideally suited to help pastors and church leaders deal with issues of organizational complexity and mission effectiveness. Today he leads a ministry that develops leadership for key churches throughout the country—*and loves doing it*. But if he had run out and followed his first adviser's counsel—if he had sold his business and simply doled out the funds—he never would have experienced the effectiveness or fulfillment that he has today.

In the Quaker tradition, a clearness committee does not come together to give you advice. (Lots of people will do that without your asking.) And it certainly does not need people who have their own agenda for your life. The primary job of this group is simply to ask questions, listen thoughtfully, and then pray for a sense from God for his calling on your life.

I need people who will help me ask questions like

—What do I enjoy doing for its own sake?
—What do I avoid doing? Why?
—For what do I wish to be remembered?
—How might the offer of money or promotion sidetrack me from my true calling?
—What would my life look like if it turned out well?

Conduct "Low-Cost Probes"

God really does take our work seriously. Arthur Miller puts it like this:

> It is *wrong*, it is *sin*, to accept or remain in a position that *you* know is a mismatch for you. Perhaps that's a form of sin you've never even considered—the sin of staying in the wrong job. But God did not place you on this earth to waste away your years in labor that does not employ his design or purpose for your life, no matter how much you may be getting paid for it.

Since discerning a calling usually requires time and patience, and most of us have bills that must be paid—what do we do while we are searching? This process is bad news for those of us who want to microwave everything, including our vocations. We may be tempted to jump into commitments too rashly.

One alternative is to conduct what Bob Buford calls a "low-cost probe." The idea is to keep your day job, but test the waters of a new calling. Begin to explore your effectiveness in the area to which you believe God may be calling you. In Bob's case, the low-cost probe began through retaining his CEO position but pulling together a group of pastors of large churches to see if they could benefit from the kind of organizational expertise he might be able to bring. This led to his finding his primary calling for the second half of his life. But the cost was low enough that, had it been a dead end, he easily could have turned his search elsewhere. Had he impulsively quit his job and taken a staff position at a church somewhere, he might have missed his calling and jeopardized his chance to keep searching.

Further, Gordon Smith notes that discernment honors previous decisions and commitments. God is a careful worker and does not waste any resources. The competencies and skills you have acquired until now matter to him and may be squandered if you leave your current situation too quickly.

Maybe for you a low-cost probe would involve a short-term mission plunge, or taking on a commitment to teach at your church, or getting involved as a volunteer launching a new ministry. Take confidence in the fact that there is biblical precedent for launching a low-cost probe. Amos transitioned into the prophecy business but still had his shepherding position to fall back on. Even Paul apparently kept his tent-making operation in production mode while he went into church planting.

A Calling Often Involves Pain

People sometimes romanticize the notion of vocation. Receiving a calling from God is not the same thing as falling into your dream career. A dream career generally promises wealth, power, status, security, and great benefits. A calling is often a different story.

God called Moses: *Go to Pharaoh—the most powerful man on earth. Tell him to let his labor force leave without compensation to worship a god he doesn't believe in. Then convince a timid, stiff-necked people to run away into the desert. That's your calling.*

And Moses said: *Here am I. Send Aaron.*

God called Jonah: *Go to Nineveh—the most corrupt and violent city in the world. Tell its inhabitants—who don't know you and won't acknowledge me—to repent or die.*

And Jonah said: *When's the next whale leaving in the opposite direction?*

God called Jeremiah to preach to people who wouldn't listen. It was so hard and Jeremiah cried so much that he became known as the Weeping Prophet. How would you like to have that job title? Who wants a business card that reads "the sobbing CEO" or "the depressed dermatologist"?

As a rule, the people whom we read about in Scripture who were called by God felt quite inadequate. When God called Abraham to leave home, or Gideon to lead an army, or Esther to defy the king, or Mary to give birth to the Messiah, their initial response was never: *Yes, I'm up to that challenge. I think I can handle that.*

The first response to a God-sized calling is generally fear. Henry Blackaby writes,

> Some people say, "God will never ask me to do something I can't do." I have come to the place in my life that, if the assignment I sense God is giving me is something that I know I can handle, I know it is probably not from God. The kind of assignments God gives in the Bible are always God-sized. They are always beyond what people can do, because he wants to demonstrate his nature, his strength, his provision, and his kindness to his people and to a watching world. This is the only way the world will come to know him.

This doesn't mean that God calls us in a way that violates our "raw material." Where God calls, God gifts.

We're not called just to work *for* God. We are called to work *with* God.

It does mean, though, that natural talent alone is not enough to honor a calling from God. I will need ideas, strength, and creativity beyond my own resources to do what God asks of me. It will have to be God and me doing it together. We are not called just to work *for* God. We are called to work *with* God.

Everyone in Scripture who said yes to their calling had to pay a high price. So will you and I.

Sometimes it will mean putting in hours of work and effort when you would rather not. Will you do it?

Maybe your calling will not involve the kind of recognition or wealth or influence you had always hoped for. Can you let that go?

Sometimes you will devote yourself to a dream—like Jeremiah—and things will not turn out the way you wanted, and you will experience crushing disappointment and discouragement. Can you persist?

Somewhere along the line, people will oppose you, disapprove of you, or block what you are trying to do. Can you endure?

Maybe it will take a long time to discern your calling. Maybe it will involve much trial and error and many false starts. And we tend to be impatient people, wanting immediate results. Will you be patient?

Having a Career Versus Having a Calling

American society does not talk much about calling anymore. It is more likely to think in terms of career. Yet, for many people a career becomes the altar on which they sacrifice their lives. Benjamin Hunnicutt is a historian who specializes in the history of work at the University of Iowa. He notes that work has become our new religion, where we worship and give our time. As people's commitment to family, community, and faith are shrinking, they begin to look to their careers to provide them with meaning, connectedness, identity, and esteem.

A calling, which is something I do *for* God, is replaced by a *career*, which threatens to *become* my god. A career is something I choose for myself; a calling is something I receive. A career is something I do for myself; a calling is something I do for God. A career promises status, money, or power; a calling generally promises difficulty and even some suffering—and the opportunity to be used by God. A career is about upward mobility; a calling generally leads to downward mobility.

When I first went into pastoral ministry, people would sometimes ask me when I got "the call," as if church work required a calling but a marketplace job was just part of a career. But that is not how it goes. I know all too well it is possible to turn church work into a career that is about advancement and achievement. It is also possible to make business a calling when it is truly done to serve God and others.

A career may end with retirement and lots of "toys." A calling isn't over until the day you die. The rewards of a career may be quite visible, but they are temporary. The significance of a calling lasts for eternity. A career can be disrupted by any number of events—but not a calling. When God calls people, he enables them to fulfill their callings even in the most unlikely circumstances.

Scripture is full of people who were pressed into slavery, captured and sent into exile, thrown into prison. Their career trajectories did not look promising, but they fulfilled their callings in extraordinary ways.

Pharaoh had a career—but Moses had a calling. Potiphar had a career—but Joseph had a calling. Haman had a career—but Esther had a calling. Ahab had a career—but Elijah had a calling. Pilate had a career—but Jesus had a calling.

And not just people in Scripture.

Charles Colson was in the midst of one of the most high-profile careers in America. He had access to power. He had enormous influence. Then he ended up in prison. He thought his career was over—and in a way he was right. His former career was finished—but his calling was just beginning. He would be called to serve men in prison just like him.

> "The real legacy of my life was my biggest failure."
>
> —Charles Colson

He would be called to serve a whole nation through both his gifts and his brokenness. He reflects, "The real legacy of my life was my biggest failure—that I was an ex-convict. My great humiliation—being sent to prison—was the beginning of God's greatest use of my life; He chose the one experience in which I could not glory for His glory."

Sometimes, in the providence of God, the end of a career is the beginning of a calling. And you have a calling. You are not a spare part—you are on a mission from God.

Just remember—there is some assembly required.

GETTING OUT OF THE BOAT

1. To what extent does your current work express your true giftedness and passion?
2. Where has impulsivity gotten you into trouble? Where have you been likely to mistake foolishness for faith?
3. Reflect on your life from childhood on: what activities and causes have brought you most internal joy and fulfillment?
4. What limitation that's part of your "raw material" is most painful to you?
5. How clear are you about your sense of calling? Try writing one or two compelling sentences to finish this phrase:
   My calling is _____

   _____

   _____

6. What is one low-cost probe you could try to explore your calling further?

He said, "Come." So Peter got out of the boat, started walking on the water, and came toward Jesus.

Matthew 14:29

Walking on the Water

I went to the woods because I wished to live delib-erately ... and not, when I came to die, discover that I had not lived.

Henry David Thoreau

Sometime ago we went on vacation to a dude ranch in Arizona. My wife, who grew up vacationing there, insisted that my experience would not be complete until I knew the exhilaration of a truly chal-lenging horse ride. We went on a trail ride, but it was far too tame to count as there was no possibility of falling and receiving a serious injury. The truth is that I have spent very little time around horses and have never actually met one I trusted, but of course I wasn't about to admit that.

So the next morning I rode out with five ranch hands to take the herd of horses to pasture about three miles away. I was very interested to meet my horse du jour. Often horses receive their name from some notable aspect of their temperament; when you get a horse named Pokey or Valium, you pretty much know what to expect. My horse was named Reverse, based on his particular eccentricity of going backward anytime someone was foolish enough to pull on his reins. I made a mental note not to do that.

The trip out to the pasture was uneventful. We dropped off the herd and were on our way back when one of the ranch hands decided to make a race of the return trip. His horse took off at full gallop and the other four immediately started racing to catch up with him. Reverse started to make his move. Instinctively, I pulled on the reins as hard as I could. Reverse rose up on his hind legs and took a few steps backward—just as Silver used to do under the Lone Ranger—and then took off like a bat out of ... a cannon.

For the better part of a mile, Reverse ran a dead heat (the word *dead* sticks in my mind). We were not sauntering or trotting—this was all-out sprinting as in a scene from a movie. The five ranch hands were college-age guys who lived on horseback all summer long, racing their horses as fast as they could. Reverse and I passed four of them. I say "Reverse and I," but the truth is, he was doing most of the work. I was just waiting to die. I was looking in the adjacent creek bed for the rock my head would split against once I was thrown off. Exodus 15:1 came to mind: "I will sing to the LORD, for he has triumphed gloriously; horse and rider he has thrown into the sea."

While I was wondering how Nancy would spend the life insurance policy, the strangest thing happened. I realized there was a good chance I would survive this, and then it became one of the most exhilarating moments I had all week. I had a few moments of what Mihaly Csikszentmihalyi calls "flow"—my own private optimal experience. For a few moments I was completely captivated by a single activity. All I could hear was the pounding of Reverse's hooves; all I could feel was the rush of the wind in my face and the swaying rhythm of the gallop. Out of the corner of my eye, I could see the startled looks of the four horsemen of the apocalypse whom we passed up (a moment I enjoyed immensely). I felt *alive*—from my now-hatless head to the toes of my stirrup-straining feet. I started laughing from sheer adrenaline. By the time we pulled up to the fence, I knew this had been the ride of my life. I would not have missed this experience for anything.

Of course, when we pulled to a stop at the ranch (which to my great relief Reverse decided to do gradually), male pride would not allow me to indicate that this dash had been at all unplanned. "Yes, a decent mount," I said. "His wind isn't quite what it could be, perhaps, but never mind."

My only choice had been to say yes or no to the ride. I had to decide whether I had enough faith to ride the horse. When I mounted that horse, I did not have a clue as to what was going to happen to me. I did not know all the details of what would happen. If I had known, I might have said no—but then I would have never known the exhilaration of the ride. Once I took a single step, once I got into the saddle, a whole world of experience was set in motion. Everything else was up to the horse. I could not control it. But I could have missed it.

Exhilaration

In some ways, the high point in the story of Peter comes in the middle of the passage. It is contained in a single phrase: *Peter . . . started walking on the water.* There are many other parts to the story—the storm; the fear that came before this and the fear that would follow; the failure and critique. These are all important parts to the story, and we learn from them because we are familiar with storms, fear, and failure. We may ignore or deny them at our peril. But they are not the whole story. In the middle of the passage is the remarkable occurrence: *Peter walked on the water.* Peter knew the joy and freedom of experiencing God's power after taking an enormous risk.

> Peter knew the joy and freedom of experiencing God's power after taking an enormous risk.

I think that during those moments Peter was storing up memories he would carry to his grave: the feel of the water somehow standing solid beneath his feet; the rush of the wind in his face; the startled looks of the boatmen as he passed them by (a moment I'll bet he enjoyed immensely). I think he knew this was the walk of his life.

I wonder what might have gone on inside Peter's mind—

I can't believe it. Nobody thought I'd actually get out of the boat—I didn't think I'd do it myself. When I let go of the side, it was the hardest thing I've ever done. I was afraid I'd die.

Yet now I find myself actually doing what Jesus is doing. I don't know how it's working—I'm not walking any differently. Yet something—Someone—is holding me up. *I think I'm beginning to understand now. It is true: He really is the One. I don't see how things can ever be the same after this. I don't see how I could ever settle for life in the boat again.*

Most especially, I think Peter was remembering the look on Jesus' face, because I suspect that Jesus beamed to see that one of his followers could trust him that far. I think, for as long as this walk lasted, that their eyes did not leave each other for an instant. Getting out of the boat was Peter's great gift to Jesus; the experience of walking on water was Jesus' great gift to Peter.

It Is Worth the Risk

Most of us love to hear messages about how powerful God is. Scripture is full of images that reassure us: He is a rock, a fortress, and a strong tower; he is a king and a warrior; he makes the clouds his chariots and rides on the wings of the wind (and I thought my ride on Reverse was exciting). We are told that God makes the earth tremble by a look, he makes the mountains smoke at a touch, and when he raises his voice the earth melts.

I love to read of how Jesus' confidence contrasted with his disciples' fear. Once, in a different boat, a tremendous storm was raging. Jesus was taking a nap even as the disciples were convinced they were going to die. When they woke him up, Jesus was not afraid at all. He just went to the side of the boat and addressed the wind: "Peace! Be still!"

Imagine being in a boat, watching a man talking to nature, then seeing a whole storm evaporate. Think they stopped being scared? Or that their fear was redirected?

Most people I know love to hear stories and images about the powerful God we serve. But here is the problem: That information alone is not sufficient enough to create courageous human beings. I can receive much information designed to assure me that God's power is sufficient. But the information alone does not transform the human heart and character. In order for such a transformation to take place, certain actions and experiences are required.

A classic example of this occurs when Moses has died, and the people are wondering if God will continue to take care of them. Repeatedly he reminds them, "Be strong and courageous; do not be frightened or dismayed, for the LORD your God is with you wherever you go."

When it is time for the Israelites to cross the River Jordan, God promises to make a way for them. They can trust him to see them across. But God asks them to take a first step: "When the soles of the feet of the priests who bear the ark of the LORD, the Lord of all the earth, rest in the waters of the Jordan, the waters of the Jordan flowing from above shall be cut off; they shall stand in a single heap."

In other words, the people will experience God's power—but they will have to take the first step. This not only involves a mental acknowledgment of God's power, but requires them to take a step of action based on the assumption that God is trustworthy as well. They had to get their feet wet first.

Here is a powerful question I first heard many years ago to help me know whether I am getting out of the boat in any area of my life: What am I doing that I could not do apart from the power of God?

> **What am I doing that I could not do apart from the power of God?**

If you were to ask Peter that question, the answer would be very simple and straightforward. It was clear that the only way Peter would be able to stay afloat was if God took over. How about you? Is there any challenge in your life right now that is large enough that you have no hope of doing it apart from God's help? If not, consider the possibility that you are seriously underchallenged.

If you want to walk on the water, you have to be willing to get your feet wet first. Then you discover it is worth the risk.

When I take the risk of giving generously, I discover that I really can trust God to take care of me—but I have to get my feet wet first.

When I take the risk of confessing a sin to another person, I discover that God really will honor truth-telling—but I have to get my feet wet first.

When I risk using my spiritual gift, I can know the joy of being used by God—but I have to get my feet wet first.

God generally helps people's faith grow by asking them to take the first step. When God called Moses to get out of the boat—to confront Pharaoh and lead his people—Moses balked. So God asked him to take a small step: "Throw down your staff." Moses did, and immediately it became a serpent. Serpents were worshiped in Egypt and were regarded as poisonous, so Moses would have been struck by the next command: "Put out your hand and pick it up—by the tail." If I were ever to pick up a poisonous serpent—which I think is altogether unlikely—I expect I would want to pick it up right behind the head. I imagine serpents can get a little testy about being picked up, and doing it by the tail gives them a lot of room to maneuver. But God wanted Moses to learn something about the first-step principle. So Moses picked up the snake, and it became a staff again. Moses discovered God was faithful. But Moses had to pick it up first. He had to take a first step.

God promised Moses and the Israelites freedom. He did deliver them from Pharaoh, but first they had to act in trust. They had to march to the Red Sea *before* he parted it.

Over and over in Scripture this pattern is repeated:

Namaan has to wash seven times in the water *before* he is cured of leprosy. Gideon must winnow his army from 32,000 down to 300 *before* God will deliver them from the Midianites. The loaves and fishes must be relinquished *before* they can be multiplied. The seed must be buried in the earth and die *before* it can be raised to greater and more fruitful life.

If I am going to experience a greater measure of God's power in my life, it will usually involve the first-step principle. It will usually begin by my acting in faith—trusting God enough to take a step of obedience. Simply acknowledging information about his power is not enough. I have to get my feet wet.

Often, at the key moments of saying yes, I don't know all the implications. No parent knows all the cost she will pay for bringing children into the world; no couple knows fully the ratio of joy or heartbreak that marriage will hold for them. It is a good thing we don't know, or we might never take that first step. But when I say yes, I set in motion an adventure that will leave me forever changed.

How Faith Grows

I believe an important reason why God so often asks us to take a first step has to do with the nature of faith and how it grows. Most people I know wish, at least at certain points in their lives, that they had more faith. I know of people who torment themselves over having too little of it. They are certain that their lack of faith is the reason for an unanswered prayer, for spiritual weakness, or for a sense of distance from God.

Martin Luther—famed as the champion of "justification by faith"—knew all about doubt.

> In Torgau a wretched little woman once came to me and said, "Ah, dear Doctor, I have the idea that I'm lost and can't be saved because I can't believe." Then I replied, "Do you believe, dear lady, that what you pray in the Creed is true?" She answered with clasped hands, "Oh yes, I believe it; it's most certainly true!" To which I replied, "Then go in God's name, dear lady. You believe more and better than I."
>
> It's the devil who puts such ideas into people's heads and says, "Ah, you must believe better. You must believe more. Your faith is not very strong and is insufficient." In this way he drives them to despair.

When people wrestle with doubt, they may tell themselves that they will try harder to have more faith. But faith is not the sort of thing that can be acquired by trying harder. Imagine if someone were to say to you, "I find myself doubting Old Faithful. I'm just not sure it can be trusted." What would your advice be? Not "Try harder to believe!" The best advice for such a person would be, "Just hang around Old Faithful. Get to know Old Faithful better." And because Old Faithful is faithful, the better you know it, the more you will trust it.

It is the same with God. Never try to have more faith—just get to know God better. And because God is faithful, the better you know

> Never try to have more faith—just get to know God better. And because God is faithful, the better you know him, the more you'll trust him.

him, the more you will trust him. The way to get to know his trust-worthiness is to risk obeying him. Ole Hallesby writes about the father who comes to Jesus to ask him to help him "if you can."

"If?" Jesus says. "All things are possible to him who believes."

"I do believe," the man says, "Help my unbelief." Like most of us, he was a mixture of trust and doubt. How much faith did he have?

"Enough to come to Jesus," Hallesby writes. "And that was enough."

How much faith do I need? Not a feeling of certainty. Just enough faith to take a step.

A Single Step

At the climax of the movie *Indiana Jones and the Last Crusade*, Indiana has to pass three supreme tests to reach the Holy Grail and save his father, who is dying. The first test is "The Breath of God." As he walks down a corridor, Indiana must bow down at precisely the right moment to keep from having his head cut off by large, revolving metal blades.

The second test is "The Word of God." Jones must walk on just the right stones—the ones that spell God's name in Latin—to keep from falling through the floor to his death.

But the third test, "The Path of God," is the most difficult. Indiana comes to the edge of a large chasm—about a hundred feet across and a thousand feet down. On the other side of the chasm is the doorway to the Holy Grail. The instructions say, "Only in the leap from the lion's head, will he prove his worth."

Indiana says to himself, "It's impossible. Nobody can jump this." Then he realizes that this test requires a leap of faith. His father says, "You must believe, boy. You must believe!" Even though every nerve and fiber of his being screams that he must not do it, Indiana walks to the edge of the cliff ... lifts his foot ... and then steps out into thin air—hoping that somehow he won't end up like Wile E. Coyote in the "Roadrunner" cartoons.

If you have seen the movie, you know what happens next. Indiana does not plummet to his death, but is upheld by an invisible force.

"Without faith it is impossible to please God," the writer of Hebrews says.

How much faith is required? Good news—not perfect certainty. Indiana Jones can have doubts—he can have a whole cavern full of them. How little confidence he feels does not count against him. And that is a good thing, because if the beads of sweat on his forehead are any indication, he is not a pillar of certainty.

He needs only enough faith to take a step. He needs only enough faith to put his life on the line. For the most part, it is a matter of the will. If he is willing to act as if a bridge will be there, the bridge will be there. He will not fall. But he has to take the step first. If he does not take the step, he will never know.

Expanding Your Spiritual Comfort Zone

Most of us have an area that might be called our "spiritual comfort zone," which is the area where we feel most comfortable trusting God. When God calls us to go beyond our spiritual comfort zone, we begin to feel nervous or uncomfortable. We would prefer not to go outside the zone until we feel better about it.

For example, we might be comfortable talking about God with church friends, but nervous about explaining our faith to someone who does not believe. We might be comfortable in our current job, but anxious about the possibility that God wants to do some vocational realignment. We might feel enough faith to pray for people we are in relationship with, but actually confronting someone who has been behaving badly toward us would make us cringe. We might discuss past problems smoothly enough, but the idea of honestly naming our current struggles to a trusted friend would send us running.

There is only one way to increase your spiritual comfort zone, and acquiring more information alone will not do it. You will have to follow the Path of God, which requires taking a leap of faith.

You need to get out of the boat a little every day. Begin the day by asking God for wisdom about where you need to get your feet wet that day. Call someone whom you have been avoiding out of fear. Express your faith to a person who does not know about your beliefs. Make a gesture of friendship toward someone when you are tempted to hold back. Risk speaking the truth to a spouse, parent, or friend when your normal course would be to hesitate. It does not matter whether all these steps turn out the way you hoped. Of course, things will end in failure sometimes, but you are giving your faith a chance to grow.

You have to get out of the boat a little every day. As you do, your faith will deepen and your spiritual comfort zone will widen.

Where is God calling you to walk on the water? Let me give you four indicators that may help you to know, and I will tell you about some real-life water-walkers along the way.

The Indicator of Fear

Very often God will ask us to step out of the boat at the point of our fears—precisely because he wants us to overcome them. For instance, one of the most exciting spiritual adventures in life is helping another human being find God. What keeps us from getting out of the boat evangelistically? The number one reason is fear. Fear of what? Historically, people have risked their livelihoods and even their lives for their faith. In many parts of the world, Christians still do. But for most of us, the worst-case scenario is that the other person will not want to talk about spiritual matters. We may experience a brief sense of embarrassment or rejection. When we ask, "Would you like to talk about spirituality?" the other person may say, "No, I don't think so. Not today. Thanks anyway." That is about the most pain we face.

On the other hand, look at the upside potential. We might actually be part of God's redemptive purposes on earth. But if I wait until I'm feeling 100 percent certain about having a spiritual conversation with somebody who is far from God, I may never have it. I will have to take the risk first. I have to get my feet wet.

> One of the most exciting spiritual adventures in life is helping another human being find God.

Jeffrey Cotter tells about one time—an unforgettable plane ride—when he took the risk. As a pastor returning from a job interview and dressed in blue jeans, he found himself sitting next to a pinstripe-wearing, attaché case–carrying, *Wall Street Journal*-reading businessman. Cotter's initial impulse was to avoid all conversation (especially about jobs), but when Mr. MBA greeted him, that option was lost. The man worked in what he called the figure salon business. He spoke of how they could change a woman's self-concept by changing her body; he talked of his excitement about the power and significance of what he did.

Cotter was struck by the man's pride in his work and accomplishments. He wondered why Christians are not more like that; why we are so often apologetic about our faith. He realized he had been in avoidance mode during the whole flight because of fear.

Looking skeptically at Cotter's clothing, Mr. MBA asked about his line of work. Let Cotter tell it from here:

> The Spirit began to brood over the face of the deep. Order and power emerged from chaos! A voice, in a whisper reminded me: "Let him who boasts, boast in the Lord."
>
> "It's interesting that we have similar business interests," I said. "You are in the body-changing business; I'm in the personality-changing business. We apply basic theocratic principles to accomplish indigenous personality modification."
>
> He was hooked, but I knew he would never admit it. (Pride is powerful.)
>
> "You know, I've heard of that," he replied hesitantly. "But do you have an office here in the city?"

"Oh, we have many offices. We have offices up and down the state. In fact, we're national; we have at least one office in every state of the union, including Alaska and Hawaii."

He had this puzzled look on his face. He was searching his mind to identify this huge company he must have read or heard about, perhaps in his *Wall Street Journal*.

"As a matter of fact, we've gone international. And Management has a plan to put at least one office in every country of the world by the end of this business era." I paused. "Do you have that in your business?"

"Well, no. Not yet," he answered. "But you mentioned management. How do they make it work?"

"It's a family concern. There's a Father and a Son ... and they run everything."

"It must take a lot of capital," he asked, skeptically.

"You mean money?" I asked. "Yes, I suppose so. No one knows just how much it takes, but we never worry because there's never a shortage. The Boss always seems to have enough. He's a very creative guy.... And the money is, well, just there. In fact, those of us in the organization have a saying about our Boss, 'He owns the cattle on a thousand hills.'"

"Oh, he's into ranching, too?" asked my captive friend.

"No, it's just a saying we use to indicate his wealth."

My friend sat back in his seat. "What about with you?" he asked.

"The employees? They're something to see," I said. "They have a 'Spirit' that pervades the organization. It works like this: The Father and Son love each other so much that their love filters down through the organization so that we all find ourselves loving one another too. I know this sounds old fashioned in a world like ours, but I have people in the organization who are willing to die for me. Do you have that in *your* business?" I was almost shouting now. People were starting to shift noticeably in their seats.

"Not yet," he said. Quickly changing strategies, he asked "But do you have good benefits?"

"They're substantial," I countered with a gleam. "I have complete life insurance, fire insurance—all the basics. You might not believe this, but it's true: I have holdings in a mansion that's being built for me right now for my retirement. Do you have that in your business?"

"Not yet" he answered wistfully. The light was dawning. "You know, one thing bothers me. I've read journals, and if your business is all that you say it is, why haven't I heard about it before now?"

"That's a good question," I said. "After all, we have a 2,000 year old tradition.... Want to sign up?"

We became more than casual strangers during those next five minutes.

Imagine having God use you to speak to another person like that. Of course, if you risk a spiritual conversation, it could go badly. You may stumble quite a lot. But if you don't take the risk, the Spirit can never use your words to touch another human soul.

Instead of letting your fear put you into avoidance mode, it may be precisely the indicator telling you where God wants to use you. But you will have to get your feet wet first to find out.

The Indicator of Frustration

Sometimes people in Scripture get motivated to trust God in remarkable ways when they grow frustrated with the brokenness of a fallen world.

Nehemiah could not tolerate the idea of Jerusalem being in ruins. He was moved to risk a king's displeasure and lethal opposition to rally God's people.

David could not tolerate a pagan Philistine giant taunting the God of Israel. He was moved to risk his life in the name of his God.

Elijah could not tolerate the barbaric practice of pagan idolatry. He was moved to take on all the prophets of Baal single-handedly.

Even in the world today, it is often at the point where we are frustrated by the gap between fallen reality and our sense of God's desires that we are moved to action in a cause greater than ourselves.

An outstanding example of this was a woman named Henrietta Mears. Miss Mears taught college-age, single young people for decades at Hollywood Presbyterian Church. She was a formative influence on the life of a whole generation of Christian leaders including Billy Graham, Bill Bright, former Senate Chaplain Richard Halverson, and hundreds of others. She was frustrated at not being able to give her students first-rate material to educate them, so she began a little publishing enterprise out of a garage. It grew into Gospel Light Publishers, one of the most effective Christian publishers of its day.

Henrietta was frustrated because she knew so many Christians living in crowded Los Angeles who needed someplace to withdraw and be with God outdoors where they could hear him better. So she drove up into the San Gabriel Mountains and found what she thought would be the perfect location. She talked to God about how much it was needed. Then she talked to the man who owned it, and although he hadn't been inclined to sell it, he never really had a prayer. It grew into Forest Home, one of the premier spiritual conference centers in the country.

Henrietta was frustrated by not having a good single-volume introduction to the Bible that could help her students understand what it was all about, so she wrote one herself that sold hundreds of thousands of copies and continues to sell today, decades after her death. She did all these things and many more, despite doing them in a day when many people thought a woman had no business doing such things. Time and again she took the step of faith, and time and again the bridge was there.

> **"I would have trusted Christ more."**
>
> —Henrietta Mears

At the end of her remarkable life, as she lay on her deathbed, someone asked her, "Miss Mears, if you had it all to do over again, would you do anything differently?"

She thought for a moment. "If I had it all to do over again—I would have trusted Christ more."

Maybe God is calling you to trust him at some point of frustration in your life. Trust him. No one ever regretted trusting Christ more—ever.

The Indicator of Compassion

Toby was the ring bearer at our wedding. He looked like a waif out of a Dickens novel—big china blue eyes, white-blond hair, skin the color of alabaster. (We promised the flower girl, who was twice his age and size, a giant piece of wedding cake if she would not let go of his hand throughout the entire ceremony. She held on to him the way a drowning man clutches a lifeline. At one point he dropped the ring pillow; she would not even relax her grip enough to let him bend down and pick it up.)

Not long after our wedding, Toby's family moved, and we lost touch. Years later, a new coworker turned out to be a good friend of Toby's family and told us what our ring bearer had been up to. When Toby was in high school, he wrote an essay on world hunger and ended up winning a two-and-a-half week study tour in Africa through World Vision.

Toby was not only struck by the beauty of Ethiopia, but also by the rampant poverty. One day during his trip, he was at a World Vision distribution camp, handing out food and supplies and playing with some of the local kids. As Toby and the other World Vision personnel were getting ready to leave, an eleven-year-old-boy tapped him on the shoulder. The boy stared at Toby's T-shirt. Then he looked down at his own shirt, which was thin, dirty, and filled with holes. He looked back at Toby and shyly asked, "Could I have your shirt?"

Toby was not prepared for that request. His luggage was a long way away, and he would not return to it all day. This would mean that he would have to go the rest of the day without a shirt in the blistering African sun. There was no time to think about what to do or say. He just backed away from the boy, shrugging his shoulders as he stepped onto the bus.

As they drove away, the weight of that one request gripped Toby and would not let him go. He continued thinking about it the rest of the day. That night, everyone in camp talked about their experiences through the day, but not Toby. He was thinking about an eleven-year-old-boy who just wanted a T-shirt. He kept thinking about what Jesus had said: "Whatever you did not do for the least of these, you did not do for me." Toby waited until everyone in the compound went to sleep, then he went back to his room and broke down and cried.

The memory of that scene haunted him the rest of the trip. Everywhere he went, Toby saw that boy's face. Even when he returned to his home in Michigan, he was not able to put it out of his mind. He thought about how we people in America have so many T-shirts, we run out of places to put them. He resolved to do something.

He organized a T-shirt drive called "Give the Shirt Off Your Back." He started collecting them door-to-door. He persuaded some 7–11 stores to set bins out for collecting the shirts. Local media outlets heard about the story and gave it some airtime. The next thing Toby knew, it seemed as if everyone in Michigan had heard about it. He collected over 10,000 T-shirts.

Then he was faced with another problem. How do you get two tons of T-shirts from Michigan to Ethiopia? He called one relief agency after another, telling them his story. He received always the same answer: "We'd like to help, but it's too expensive." How expensive? He called United Parcel Service and asked how much it would cost to send two tons of T-shirts to Africa: The response: $65,000.

So Toby prayed some more. "Okay, God, *you* raised up these shirts. Now how are you going to get them where they belong?"

Finally, Toby was put in touch with an outfit called Supporters of Sub-Sahara Africa. They happened to be taking a shipment of supplies to Africa and agreed to take his T-shirts along for the ride. There was just one hitch: They could take them to only one country. Would it be all right, they wanted to know, if the shirts went to Ethiopia?

Toby does not know exactly where the T-shirts ended up, but he hopes one of them ended up in the hands of a certain boy. "I'll never forget that kid," he says. "I know it's unlikely he'll get one of the shirts I sent. What are the odds of that? But I can pray. God can do *anything*."

Maybe a strong surge of compassion is how God will indicate to you that he wants you to walk on the water. When is the last time you took a serious compassion risk? Jesus did this all the time—touching lepers, eating with tax collectors, and hanging out with prostitutes was an avocation with him. Maybe for you it will mean getting involved with Big Brothers or doing short-term volunteer relief work in a Third

World country. Maybe it will mean taking the time to have compassion on somebody who works in an office down from you or lives in a house on your block.

The Indicator of Prayer

It is striking to me how—both in Scripture and in present-day examples—stories of water-walking are almost always stories about prayer. There is something about getting out of the boat that turns people into intense pray-ers, because they are aware that they cannot accomplish things without God's help.

One of my favorite adventures in prayer involves Doug Coe, who has a ministry in Washington, D.C., that mostly involves people in politics and statecraft. Doug became acquainted with Bob, an insurance salesman who was completely unconnected with any government circles. Bob became a Christian and began to meet with Doug to learn about his new faith.

One day, Bob came in all excited about a statement in the Bible where Jesus says, "Ask whatever you will in my name, and you shall receive it."

"Is that really true?" Bob demanded.

Doug explained, "Well, it's not a blank check. You have to take it in context of the teachings of the whole Scripture on prayer. But yes—it really is true. Jesus really does answer prayer."

"Great!" Bob said. "Then I gotta start praying for something. I think I'll pray for Africa."

"That's kind of a broad target. Why don't you narrow it down to one country?" Doug advised.

"All right. I'll pray for Kenya."

"Do you know anyone in Kenya?" Doug asked.

"No."

"Ever been to Kenya?"

"No." Bob just wanted to pray for Kenya.

So Doug made an unusual arrangement. He challenged Bob to pray every day for six months for Kenya. If Bob would do that and nothing extraordinary happened, Doug would pay him five hundred dollars. But if something remarkable did happen, Bob would pay Doug five hundred dollars. And if Bob did not pray every day, the whole deal was off. It was a pretty unusual prayer program, but then Doug is a creative guy.

Bob began to pray, and for a long while nothing happened. Then one night he was at a dinner in Washington. The people around the table explained what they did for a living. One woman said she helped run an orphanage in Kenya—the largest of its kind.

Bob saw five hundred dollars suddenly sprout wings and begin to fly away. But he could not keep quiet. Bob roared to life. He had not said much up to this point, and now he pounded her relentlessly with question after question.

"You're obviously very interested in my country," the woman said to Bob, overwhelmed by his sudden barrage of questions. "You've been to Kenya before?"

"No."

"You know someone in Kenya?"

"No."

"Then how do you happen to be so curious?"

"Well, someone is kind of paying me five hundred dollars to pray...."

She asked Bob if he would like to come visit Kenya and tour the orphanage. Bob was so eager to go, he would have left that very night if he could.

When Bob arrived in Kenya, he was appalled by the poverty and the lack of basic health care. Upon returning to Washington, he couldn't get this place out of his mind. He began to write to large pharmaceutical companies, describing to them the vast need he had seen. He reminded them that every year they would throw away large amounts of medical supplies that went unsold. "Why not send them to this place in Kenya?" he asked.

And some of them did. This orphanage received more than a million dollars' worth of medical supplies.

The woman called Bob up and said, "Bob, this is amazing! We've had the most phenomenal gifts because of the letters you wrote. We would like to fly you back over and have a big party. Will you come?"

So Bob flew back to Kenya. While he was there, the president of Kenya came to the celebration, because it was the largest orphanage in the country, and offered to take Bob on a tour of Nairobi, the capital city. In the course of the tour they saw a prison. Bob asked about a group of prisoners there.

"They're political prisoners," he was told.

"That's a bad idea," Bob said brightly. "You should let them out."

Bob finished the tour and flew back home. Sometime later, Bob received a phone call from the State Department of the United States government:

"Is this Bob?"

"Yes."

"Were you recently in Kenya?"

"Yes."

"Did you make any statements to the president about political prisoners?"

"Yes."

"What did you say?"

"I told him he should let them out."

The State Department official explained that the department had been working for years to get the release of these prisoners, to no avail. Normal diplomatic channels and political maneuverings had led to a dead end. But now the prisoners had been released, and the State Department was told it had been largely because of ... Bob. So the government was calling to say thanks.

Several months later, the president of Kenya made a phone call to Bob. He was going to rearrange his government and select a new cabinet. Would Bob be willing to fly over and pray for him for three days while he worked on this very important task?

So Bob—who was not politically connected at all—boarded a plane once more and flew back to Kenya, where he prayed and asked God to give wisdom for the leader of the nation as he selected his government. All this happened because one man got out of the boat.

How about you? What are you praying for? Give it six months. I'll make you a deal—I'll give you the Bob Challenge. If you pray every day for six months and nothing extraordinary happens, write me. I won't promise you five hundred dollars, but I will give you a refund on the cost of this book. To the contrary, if something extraordinary does happen, you have to write and tell me about it.

Walking on the water is not about some great thing you will do. In fact, by yourself you can do nothing of lasting value. It is about what God longs to do with you by his power and grace.

But first you have to get your feet wet.

GETTING OUT OF THE BOAT

1. When have you most vividly experienced God at work in and through you—"walking on the water"? Describe what it was like.
2. How would you answer this: "What am I doing today that I could not do apart from the power of God?"
3. "Never try to have more faith. Instead, just get to know God better." How would you describe your faith these days? What might help you get to know God better?
4. What is one step you could take today to expand your "spiritual comfort zone"?
5. What about Bob? What one area of the world, or one cause, or one need that's bigger than yourself would you be willing to pray for over the next six months?

But when he noticed the strong wind, he became frightened, and beginning to sink, he cried out, "Lord, save me!" Jesus immediately reached out his hand and caught him, saying to him, "You of little faith, why did you doubt?" When they got into the boat, the wind ceased.

Matthew 14:30–32

Seeing the Wind

Jesus promised those who would follow him only three things ... that they would be absurdly happy, entirely fearless, and always in trouble.

Gregg Levoy

Undaunted Courage is Stephen Ambrose's best-selling account of the Lewis and Clark expedition. After two years of battling nearly insurmountable problems—hunger, fatigue, desertion, hostile enemies, severe illness, and death—the party had reached the headwaters of the Missouri River. All their advance information had led them to believe that once they reached the continental divide, they would face about a half-day portage, and then reach the waters of the Columbia River and float safely to the Pacific Ocean. They were on their way to hero status. The hard part was behind them. Or so they thought.

Meriwether Lewis left the rest of his party behind to climb the bluffs that would enable him to see the other side, hoping to see the waters that would carry them the rest of the way. Imagine what he felt when, rather than seeing a gentle sloping valley as expected, he was instead the first non-Native American to lay eyes on the Rocky Mountains!

What do you do when you think your biggest problems are behind you, only to find out you have just been warming up? How do you rally the rest of the troops? I picture Lewis motioning the rest of his party to stay behind a little longer while he tries to figure out how to break the news: *Hang on a minute, guys. Don't come up yet. I have a little surprise for you.*

Eventually, crossing the Rocky Mountains would be perhaps the supreme achievement of the whole trip. This challenge would call forth enormous creativity and perseverance; it would lead them to spectacular sights and unforgettable memories; it would build tremendous confidence because when they had tackled the Rocky Mountains, they would know they could tackle anything.

But on this side of the Rockies, of course, they could not know any of that yet. All they knew was that when they were hoping for a downstream ride, they had to climb their highest mountain.

Peter was on his way to hero status. The hard part was behind him—getting out of the boat. He was mastering this water-walking business. Then it happened—reality set in. As his initial enthusiasm subsided, he realized just how bad the storm was. "He saw the wind."

This detail intrigues me. I would think that once Peter was actually experiencing the sensation of walking on the water, then whether the surface was smooth or choppy would not make a great deal of difference. The normal laws of physics would already be pretty much inoperable anyway. But Matthew apparently wants us to understand that even for someone who has walked in faith for a while, storms can be a disruptive business. Peter saw the wind.

The same thing happens to us. We launch into a great adventure—start a new job, take on a stretching ministry assignment, begin a family. In the initial days we are filled with hope. We are out of the boat! We are on the way to hero status, or at least achieving something worthwhile.

Then reality sets in. We see the wind. We face obstacles. Unexpected conflict saps our spirit. Plans go awry. People we were counting on let us down. The economy zigs when it should have zagged. Just when we were hoping for easy portage and smooth sailing, we are looking at the Rocky Mountains. What happens next?

Here is where things get interesting. There is a field in the social sciences that explores what has come to be known as resiliency. Researchers study people who have survived traumatic ordeals—when life did not turn out the way they planned. Some of the classic cases involved 3,000 prisoners of war who returned from "brainwashing" experiences in Korea, 550 men who lived through captivity in Vietnam, and 52 hostages released after fourteen months of imprisonment in Iran. Other studies include survivors of World War II concentration camps, victims of crippling accidents, and children from very difficult backgrounds.

These studies have found that people generally respond to traumatic problems in one of two ways. Many are simply defeated by such difficult conditions, as we might expect. But some are marked by *resiliency*, a condition whereby they actually enlarge their capacity to handle problems and, in the end, not only survive but grow. What makes the difference? How do you endure in the face of a storm? Why do the Rockies energize some people and defeat others?

The answers have centered on a few themes:

—Resilient people continually seek to reassert some command and control over their destiny rather than seeing themselves as passive victims.
—Resilient people have a larger than usual capacity for what might be called moral courage—for refusing to betray their values.
—Resilient people find purpose and meaning in their suffering.

For those who seek to water-walk in wisdom—what we called the Type W personality in chapter 3—these qualities are not just the product of a strong character. Each one of them grows out of a deep dependence on God. So let's take a look at a storm facer and mountain climber in Scripture by the name of Joseph. First we will find out how he was introduced to the Rockies. Then we will see how three qualities gave him a remarkably resilient faith.

Good News/Bad News

Growing up, I always liked good news/bad news stories—where details keep turning the story from triumph to tragedy and back.

(You know the kind I mean: Two baseball-loving friends agree that whichever one dies first will come back and let the other know if there's baseball in heaven. The first one to die contacts his friend and says, "The good news is that there is baseball in heaven. The bad news is that you're pitching Friday.")

Joseph's life is about to become a good news/bad news story.

Joseph is his daddy's favorite: That's very good.

But his brothers hate his guts: That's very bad.

His daddy gives him a beautiful coat: That's very good.

But his brothers rip it off, cover it with blood, pretend he's dead, sell him into slavery in a distant land: That's very bad.

He lands a job in Egypt's Silicon Valley working for Potiphar—a wealthy, not-too-bright boss with a laissez-faire management style. Potiphar likes him, so Joseph is extremely empowered. He's promoted to work in the front office and ends up in charge of everything—he is on the cover of *Forbes* and *Business Week*. Plus, he's a strikingly handsome man, sort of like Tom Cruise, but taller and better-looking. This is all very good.

Potiphar's wife thinks he's good-looking and tries to seduce him. This is very bad.

Joseph resists. Very good.

But the wife is furious. She lies to her husband and gets Joseph arrested. Since Egypt does not have good sexual harassment legislation on the papyrus at this time, Joseph is shafted. Very bad.

In prison Joseph meets Pharaoh's butler, interprets a dream that predicts the butler will get paroled, and arranges for the butler to get Joseph's release. Very, very good.

But the butler forgets, and Joseph languishes in prison. Very, very bad.

We wonder: How will it end? What matters in any good news/bad news story is the last turn. How does it end? If it ends with bad news, all the good that went before it is just a cruel farce that raises false hopes. If it ends with good news, the entire story gets redeemed. All bad news is seen in a new light. But we have to go to the beginning.

Wearing the Robe

Joseph wore the Robe. The Robe said he was the chosen one—the golden boy. It meant he never had to wonder if his father loved him. It was the promise of a charmed life.

When his brothers walked into the room, their dad might ask them how the flocks were doing or if they had completed their tasks. When Joseph walked into the room, Jacob's eyes would light up and his face would beam. Joseph was the one their dad bragged about. Joseph got to stay up later, play longer, work less, and get away with more than any of them. Jacob knew how Joseph was doing in school and what his friends' names were. Jacob was a little fuzzy about the details of his other sons' lives.

In a hundred ways—ways that most parents are not even aware of, but kids see a mile away—Jacob's favoritism for Joseph leaked out of him. One day, though, it took a most concrete form: He gave Joseph the Robe.

The Hebrew word to describe this garment is uncertain—"a long coat with sleeves," some translations put it. The Greek translation of the Old Testament—the Septuagint—called it the "coat of many colors;" and that is what the King James Version says, and that is how it looks in most of our imaginations.

Joseph received a hand-tailored coat from Nordstroms while the rest of the boys got their clothes off the rack at K-mart—when the blue light was flashing. You don't clothe twelve growing boys on a nomad's salary without watching the budget. But when it came to Joseph, the son of his old age, Jacob splurged. Joseph wore the Robe.

What made the coat an explosive matter in the family was not just that it was expensive and made out of nice material. In those days, clothing was an expression of status. Purple was reserved for kings—a statement of royalty. This robe marks Joseph as his father's pet. This is an open, visible, in-your-face expression of raw favoritism.

Joseph wears the Robe quite often—it makes him feel special. It feels like a promise, perhaps, that he will never be alone, that he will never be merely "normal," that he will always have his father's protection and will be spared the problems others face. But every time he wears it, it is a reminder to his brothers that they will never be loved by their father the way Joseph is loved. Every time he wears it, they die a little inside.

That beautiful robe becomes a death shroud for the family. One day his brothers decide they cannot endure it for another day, so they tear the Robe off Joseph and sell him into slavery. He is just in the foothills—the Rockies are still ahead. Joseph's problems are just beginning. Joseph is about to get a front-row look at the wind.

Powerful Dreams

Joseph not only wore the Robe but also dreamed big dreams of his destiny. Dreams in that day were generally considered prophetic, though it is interesting that the writer does not say Joseph's are from God. These are striking dreams about Joseph's future, and you'd think that he might have the common sense to keep quiet. But he does not. Instead, he gathers his brothers—who don't have a special robe like his, who have been desperately hurt by his father, and who hate him—and tells them about his dream. (If you have siblings, imagine this happening in your family!)

Listen to my dream, Joseph tells them. There was a field of sheaves, when suddenly my sheaf rose and stood upright, and all your sheaves gathered around and bowed down to mine. This means one day I will rule over all of you. I will command; you will submit. You will bow down in humble expression of your obedience to my authority. Isn't that cool? Aren't you happy for me? Let's play "bow down sheaf " now to practice.

The writer makes their response very clear: "So they hated him even more because of his dreams and his words." Serious sheaf envy.

Then Joseph has another dream. You'd think that by now he has learned to keep his dreams to himself. But he is so captivated by his dreams that the thought apparently does not cross his mind.

He is going to accomplish great things. He is going to be famous. He is going to make his father proud. He is going to do a little water-walking. Joseph wears the Robe.

Facing the Storm

Then one day Joseph was attacked by his brothers, sold to a traveling caravan, carried off to a distant land, and purchased as a slave by a family he did not know.

Joseph saw the wind.

Penniless, powerless, friendless, homeless—he was about to learn what each of us sooner or later comes to know: Your heart is revealed and your character is forged when life does not turn out the way you planned. It is hard enough to get out of the boat when the wind is calm and the water's smooth. But in life that is rarely the case. Sooner or later the storm strikes—in your marriage, work, ministry, finances, or health. It is in the act of facing the storm that you discover what lies inside you and decide what lies before you.

What are the key decisions that the storm forces?

Resilient People Exercise Control Rather Than Passively Resign

their right to choose

A major theme that characterizes resilient persons is their surprising exercise of control in a stress-filled environment. Many POWs and hostages report that the single most stressful aspect of their ordeal was the realization that they had lost command over their existence. Those who lapsed into a state of passive acceptance—what observers of the Korean prison camps of the 1950s called "give-up-itis"—were the least likely to survive and recover. Amazingly enough, losing control over their daily lives was more critical to their psychological well-being than their more obvious sufferings—threats, hunger, beatings, and isolation.

In contrast, the POWs and hostages who triumphed over adversity share a common trait—they managed to reassert a sense of command over their future. Instead of becoming passive, they focused as much attention as possible on whatever possibilities for control remained.

This held true for Vietnam POWs. Prisoners would place themselves on strenuous exercise regimens, memorize stories, or invent new games. Some ordered their time by keeping a careful census of insects in their cell. They ingeniously defied their captives' orders not to communicate with each other. Some of them developed secret signals such as taps on the wall that stood for letters of the alphabet. One prisoner used strokes of his broom to send messages in code; another sent messages by dragging his sandal. Thus, the POWs encouraged each other and reminded themselves that their bodies had been captured but their spirits had not.

Joseph, too, is a prisoner—far from home, separated from his father, betrayed by his own brothers, surrounded by strangers who bought and sold him. His robe is long gone—stolen by his brothers, ripped to shreds, covered with blood, and presented to Jacob as evidence of

Joseph's death. His robe—and the charmed life it once stood for—is just a memory now.

But it is precisely at the time when the storm hits that the writer makes the most striking statement he will ever make about Joseph—the most striking thing that could ever be said about any human being.

Far from home, separated from his father, betrayed by his brothers, kidnapped by slave-traders, surrounded by strangers—the writer says, "The LORD was with Joseph." Imagine what happened to his courage and confidence when he found out that after the worst had happened to him, it led to the best! The Lord was with Joseph. He could face the Rockies after all!

Even though he had lost his freedom, Joseph refused to think of himself as powerless. He began to show remarkable amounts of initiative and autonomy—because the Lord was with him.

The Scriptures in fact have a quite thorough account of POWs and hostages who refused passivity.

Daniel in exile took control of his diet: "But Daniel resolved that he would not defile himself with the royal rations of food and wine."

Peter and the other apostles refused to accept a gag order against preaching the gospel as a Get-Out-of-Jail-Free Card.

Paul and Silas took control of their time by holding a sing-along: "About midnight Paul and Silas were praying and singing hymns to God, and the prisoners were listening to them"—as if the other prisoners had a choice!

Faith believes that with God, we are never helpless victims.

Even though it wasn't his dream, even though his dream seemed dead, Joseph applied himself diligently to the task at hand. I would have been tempted to give up: *This isn't what I'd signed up for. I may have to work for Potiphar, but I don't have to like it.* But Joseph, even though a slave, worked hard to please both master and Lord.

> But Joseph, even though a slave, worked hard to please both Master and Lord.

There is a progression in the story. We are told that Joseph was "in the house," meaning that he was not simply a worker in the field. He had been promoted to work in the house. He was management.

Then the text says, "Joseph found favor in his [Potiphar's] sight and attended him"—now he is executive assistant. After this, Potiphar names him overseer; Joseph becomes CEO of the whole operation. Potiphar's trust is so complete that he never even asks to look at the books. "So he left all that he had in Joseph's charge; and, with him there, he had no concern for anything but the food that he ate." Denny's or Chili's tonight? Soup or salad?

Because Joseph did not quit, he set in motion the development of his potential—the deepening of his faith and endurance—that would one day enable him to become the most effective leader in Egypt and fulfill the part God intended for him to play in the rescue of his family and the redemption of the world.

What if Joseph had lived in a spirit of passive resignation? He would have missed his destiny. Quitting is always easier than enduring. It is always easier to stop and have a donut than to run another lap, or to stomp out of a room in anger than to stay and seek to resolve the conflict.

When life does not turn out the way you had planned, the option of quitting will always begin to look like sweet relief:

—"This marriage is difficult, I just want out. Or, even if I don't seek an outright divorce, I'll just settle for mediocrity. I'll quit trying."

—"Seeking to live on a budget and honor God with a tithe is just too hard. I'm going to spend!"

—"This job or this ministry is not what I'd dreamed of. I had planned on doing *great* things, playing on a bigger field—not having to be faithful in *this* situation. I think I'll bail out."

Someone once asked a desert father named Abba Anthony, "What must one do to please God?" The first two pieces of advice were expected: Always be aware of God's presence, and always obey God's Word. But the third was surprising: "Wherever you find yourself—do not easily leave." The idea was that community is hard, authentic friendship is hard, patience in work is hard—so leaving will always look more attractive in the short run. But over the long haul, leaving easily has a tendency to produce people who live in a pattern of giving up. *Do not easily leave.*

Growth happens when you seek or exert control where you are able to rather than giving up in difficult circumstances. It happens when you decide to be wholly faithful in a situation that you do not like and cannot understand. It happens when you keep walking even though you see the wind. Then you discover that, somehow, you are not alone. As he was with Joseph, the Lord is also with you.

At any rate, Joseph finds himself a stranger and a slave, but he endures and rises to the top of the organization chart. It seems to us that the bad news should be over.

But then he runs into trouble of another kind. Potiphar's wife "cast her eyes on Joseph" and said to him, "Lie with me." This is not a subtle approach. It brings us to another crossroad.

Resilient People Remain Committed to Their Values When Tempted to Compromise

Now Joseph must wrestle with temptation. At least, we assume he is tempted. Although the text tells us that Joseph was a looker, it never actually gets around to describing Potiphar's wife. She may have looked like Jabba the Hut for all we know, in which case Joseph's running away takes on an entirely different flavor. But in every preacher's version of this story I have ever heard, she is described more along the lines of a super model; perhaps because it makes for a juicier story. At any rate, I am going to assume that in his loneliness Joseph was tempted.

Joseph could have thought, *Where is God? I'm far from home, hated by my brothers, isolated from my father. I wore the Robe, but now I'm a slave, and a slave is all I'll ever be. I'll never have what my father has, what I dreamed of having, what I deserve to have—my own life, wife, family, property, and name. Why shouldn't I reach for what little happiness I can get? It's not like I have anything to lose.*

But Joseph says no.

He speaks of the trust that Potiphar has placed in him and about the significance of honoring trust. His life and world are given meaning by loyalty and honoring relational commitment. To follow another way would be to enter a world of darkness that would destroy life as he knows it.

This is a classic case of resilient thinking. One reason why the American public was fascinated by candidate John McCain's biography in the 2000 presidential campaign is the account of how he could have been released by Hanoi as a POW, but refused to go unless his comrades were freed as well. Loyalty to values even when it means suffering is a powerful catalyst for character formation.

Potiphar's wife persists: "And although she spoke to Joseph day after day, he would not consent to lie beside her or to be with her." The implication of that last phrase is that she may have moderated her demand in hopes of getting Joseph to take the first step—just a small step over the line. "Let's just be together for a while. Just be with me." She wants Joseph to be with her, revel in her attentiveness and flattery, make fun of her husband as she does, exchange glances and notes and touches that are full of promise until, eventually, they would cross the final line.

Still Joseph refuses.

Finally she decides to force the issue:

> One day, however, when he went into the house to do his work, and while no one else was in the house, she caught hold of his garment, saying, "Lie with me!" But he left his garment in her hand, and fled and ran outside.

There are times, when life does not turn out the way you planned and temptation has a very strong hold on your garment, when the only thing to do is run.

Sometime ago we were eating dinner with some friends in their backyard. They had a blue light set up, and periodically we would hear a ZZZZZap sound buzzing in the night. We asked what it was.

"It's the sound of bugs hitting a bug zapper. The light attracts them, they fly in and get zapped."

It went on all night long—hundreds and hundreds of bugs. You would think that after a while the bugs would wise up. You would think they would observe that the tray underneath the light is littered with the bodies of impulsive relatives who went before them. You would think some thoughtful bug would say, "Whoa—wait a minute! I'm not going to just blindly follow my desires. I notice all my friends get drawn into this, but they never come back. I'm going to consider just how high a price I'm willing to pay for the experience of a close look at the beautiful big blue light."

But no bug ever does this. Apparently they say to themselves, "I know what I'm doing. I'm strong enough, smart enough to handle this attraction without getting burned. I'm not going to pause for reflection—I'm a buzzzzzy guy."

All night long it went on—zap, zap, zap.

Sometimes I wonder if we are any smarter. It may be that you have experienced the temptation that comes when life does not turn out the way you planned. Sin that at another point in your life you would have spurned instead begins to look attractive. Little rationalizations play themselves out in your mind.

C. S. Lewis wrote in *The Screwtape Letters* that although we would think people are most vulnerable to temptation in seasons when their energy level and appetites are highest, in fact it is when we are in the valley, when we are struck by sadness or desolation, that we are in the most dangerous place.

Sin, to paraphrase what psychologist Carl Jung once said about neurosis, is always a substitute for legitimate suffering. It is an attempt to obtain the pleasure that does not rightfully belong to me or evade the pain that does.

Problems and discouragement are the blue light that make sin appear irresistible. I know I am never more subject to temptation than in those times when life does not turn out the way I planned. I came home from work on a day when things did not go well. I wondered if I was in the right place, doing the right thing. I felt anxious about the future. My wife and I were driving to dinner, and our two daughters— then ages seven and five—continued squabbling about who has violated whose airspace even after I warned them to stop. I turned around and began yelling at them with a rage that silenced everyone in the car. I knew the anger was harmful, I knew it was all out of proportion to what they had done, yet I didn't stop. I didn't want to stop. It felt powerful and strong. But when I finished, I saw a look of fear in those little eyes that haunted me. I wondered where all that anger came from and why I could unleash it on such unsuspecting targets, whom I love so much. I realized that I would rather feel a surge of power from misplaced rage than face the truth about my anxieties and pain about my day, my future.

A friend of mine, an executive, told me about a business trip that did not go well. An account that he thought he had sewn up went horribly wrong. Sitting in a hotel lounge, lamenting his failure, lonely and bored, he was unexpectedly approached by "Potiphar's wife." A temptation that he would normally not have given a second glance suddenly felt irresistible.

A student on a playground has known the pain of rejection his whole life. He is one day magically invited into the inner circle of acceptance and being chosen, but only on one condition: He must join in the rejection and humiliation of the one person lower on the social register than he—his only friend.

These people all know the temptation of Joseph, the temptation that comes when life does not turn out the way they planned. If Joseph had given in here, he would have betrayed the one who trusted him, would have betrayed God, and would probably never have known his destiny. Instead, he ran. We know what he ran away from—from Potiphar's wife, from Ms. Temptation beckoning him to the blue light. We are told that he ran outside, but I wonder if when he got outside he found himself running to God. I wonder if he did not pour out his heart—all the disappointment and aloneness that made temptation so painful. I don't think it is ever enough just to run away from sin. Sin is a pretty dogged pursuer. Sooner or later, you have to turn and face the pain that makes the temptation so attractive. Sooner or later, you have to run to God.

> Sooner or later, you have to turn and face the pain that makes the temptation so attractive. Sooner or later, you have to run to God.

At any rate, Joseph stands firm. He is loyal to his employer, forthright with his would-be seductress, and true to his values. Now God will surely have to reward him—right?

Mrs. Potiphar stands there with his garment in her hand. Once more Joseph will be stripped of his robe and have it used against him.

She calls to the household, "See, my husband has brought among us a Hebrew to insult us. He came in to lie with me, and I cried out in a loud voice; and when he heard me raise my voice and cry out, he left his garment beside me and fled outside." She cleverly manipulates the household by appealing to their hostility toward slaves and foreigners, then lies to her husband and implies that Joseph tried to rape her.

We read this and think to ourselves, "This can't be! God's not going to let Mrs. Potiphar get away with it—is he? If he's any kind of God, the truth must come out. Potiphar must see through this floozy. Joseph must be rewarded."

Not quite. Potiphar goes on the warpath, Joseph goes to prison, and Mrs. Potiphar goes home, presumably to wait for a more compliant slave.

We are not to the end of the story yet. There's more bad news. But in the middle of the bad news comes a familiar phrase: "The LORD was with Joseph and showed him steadfast love; he gave him favor in the sight of the chief jailer."

The Lord did not spare Joseph from prison. The Lord often does not seem to spare his children much. But the Lord was there with him—as he is with you. Joseph decided he would rather face life with the Lord and have nothing than face life without the Lord and have everything. And here we see another remarkable facet of his life.

Resilient People Find Meaning and Purpose in the Storm

Victor Frankl was a Viennese psychiatrist who survived the Nazi death camps at Auschwitz and Treblinka. He discovered that the imprisoned person who no longer had a goal was unlikely to survive. His work led him to the conclusion that what he titled "Man's Search for Meaning" was in fact the primary force in life.

We who lived in concentration camps can remember the men who walked through the huts comforting others, giving away their last piece of bread. They may have been few in number, but they offer sufficient proof that everything can be taken away from a man but one thing: the last of the human freedoms—to choose one's attitude in any given set of circumstances, to choose one's way. The way in which a man accepts his fate and all the suffering that it entails, the way in which he takes up his cross, gives him ample opportunity—even in the most difficult circumstances—to add a deeper meaning to his life.

Similarly, Warsaw psychiatrist Adam Szymusik found that survivors who had taken no strong convictions into the camps with them did not fare as well over time as those who felt they suffered for their political or religious views. Studies of suicide notes have found that they rarely mention problems like failing health, rejection, or financial crises. Rather, they speak of being "tired of life" with suicide as "a way out." As psychologist Julius Segal puts it, "Countless individuals beset by trauma report that their basic problem is an existence that is without meaning."

We know that Joseph, even in prison, was filled with meaning and purpose: "But the Lord was with Joseph...." To use the language of theophany, the Lord wanted to pass by Joseph—in prison!

David Garland observes that theophanies are usually set on mountaintops. Traditionally, people encounter God in these breathtaking vistas where vision is unlimited and they are far removed from the routines of the world. Moses had a mountaintop encounter, as did Elijah. The Transfiguration happened on a mountain.

But every once in a while, as a change of pace, God will give someone a theophany in the middle of the sea. The sea was regarded by Israelites as a place of dangerous storms and sinister power. It is ranked in Revelation along with death and Hades as a place that will one day have to "give up their dead." Sometimes God comes, not in those moments when we are most lifted up, but when we are down the lowest in the place of vulnerability and fear. Sometimes he comes, not on the mountaintop, but in the storm. So it was for the disciples in the boat. So it was for Joseph.

> But the LORD was with Joseph and showed him steadfast love; he gave him favor in the sight of the chief jailer. The chief jailer committed to Joseph's care all the prisoners who were in the prison, and whatever was done there, he was the one who did it.

In prison Joseph initially found meaning in a very simple way—by helping a couple of cell mates, a baker and a butler. One morning, after they had troubling dreams, we're told, "When Joseph came to them in the morning, he *saw* that they were troubled. So he asked Pharaoh's officers, who were with him under house arrest, 'Why are your faces downcast today?'"

This is a striking detail in the story. It would be easy for Joseph to become isolated, to focus only on his own disappointment. When life does not turn out the way you plan, you forget that other people face disappointment too. You may begin to think only about your own hurts. Your world becomes so small that your pain is the only pain you notice. This is the death of the heart, the loss of meaning.

Instead, Joseph realizes that he is not the only one for whom life has not turned out according to plan. He lives the way Jesus would. He treats disgraced prisoners like human beings—he notices them, asks about them, and expresses genuine interest in them.

At a time when we would expect him to be self-preoccupied, Joseph is sincerely concerned for others' well-being: "Why are your faces downcast today?" He does this even though he is not expecting anything in return. And by his noticing, Joseph gives meaning to his presence in prison.

I wonder if part of the meaning of Joseph's suffering was to develop his compassion. That is not to say that all human suffering is merely a moral object lesson from God—I think that kind of theology trivializes human tragedy and blasphemes God's character. But I wonder if Joseph didn't need to face a storm or two.

Joseph was the golden boy, and he wore the Robe. But it can be a hard thing to wear the robe of favoritism and expectations. It damaged the brothers who were deprived, yet I wonder if it damaged Joseph as well. When you are the golden child and expect to lead a charmed life, some bad things can happen:

—You may grow up with a need to be the big sheaf among smaller, submissive sheaves. When someone else comes along who is smarter, more powerful, or more attractive— you don't like it. You want to be the one to wear the Robe.

—You may become insensitive to the way your power and status affect others.

—Beneath that robe may lurk the fear that you will lose your favored position. Then who would you be?

It may have been no accident that Joseph spent years as a slave and then as a prisoner in jail before he was ready to be exalted to a prominent position and be used by God. Storms have a way of teaching what nothing else can. As Scott Peck puts it, "It is in this whole process of meeting and solving problems that life has its meaning.... It is only because of problems that we grow mentally and spiritually.... It is for this reason that wise people learn not to dread but actually to welcome problems and actually to welcome the pain of problems."

> Storms have a way of teaching what nothing else can.

David Weiner, in a book nicely titled *Battling the Inner Dummy*, speaks about what he calls "controlled trauma" to induce transformation. We recognize that traumatic events can change our lives, for better or for worse. They can bring about deep character and personality change. Boot camp, for example, can be thought of as an example of controlled trauma that is designed to foster traits like loyalty and obedience. Allowing his disciples to face a storm alone in a boat is an example of Jesus using controlled trauma with masterful skill to help them take the step toward trust that they would never be able to develop on their own. It may be that Joseph needed a little controlled trauma in his life.

As long as he was wearing the Robe, Joseph could never enter into community with his brothers. As long as he was wearing the Robe, Joseph would never know what he was capable of under adversity. As long as he was wearing the Robe, Joseph would never understand that God is enough even when you have lost everything.

In any event, whether it was deliberately sent in order to teach Joseph something or whether it was simply a result of living in a fallen world, the storm hit. Joseph learned what life was like without the Robe. When he was home, he never seemed to notice how his grandiose dreams and exalted status affected his brothers. But now, in prison, he *noticed*. His suffering gave him eyes of compassion.

How Compassionate Are Your Actions?

In the midst of the storm, do you read the faces of people around you the way Joseph did? Most people wear on their faces what is going on inside of them.

Do you look at your friends, coworkers, people who serve you, or children in your life, and *notice* if their faces are downcast? It is a paradox: Self-preoccupation is actually self-defeating and produces loneliness.

Joseph expressed his heart to his fellow prisoners in a single question: "Why are your faces downcast today?"

Someone noticed them. Someone cared about their lives. Words can do this. Every word you speak boosts someone's hope a bit, or kills it just a little.

I was speaking at an out-of-state conference, and one of the attendees approached me and said, "I recognize your voice. I've heard it before. I have a friend who gets all your tapes from your church, and he sends me the *good ones*." I didn't have the heart to ask what percentage that might be.

Here's a little test: During the stormy periods in your life, how often have you expressed genuine concern when you have had nothing to gain?

The prisoners explain to Joseph that each of them has had a troubling dream. Joseph takes a moment to offer help: "Do not interpretations belong to God? Please tell them to me."

The butler tells of his dream about a vine and grapes. Joseph replies, "Within three days Pharaoh will lift up your head and restore you to your office."

The baker is greatly encouraged by this and shares his dream about birds and cakes. Joseph replies, "Within three days Pharaoh will lift up your head—*from you!*—and hang you on a pole."

And the baker says, "That's the last time I tell you one of my dreams."

The butler is released. This is good news. Joseph has arranged for the butler to speak a good word in his behalf, to get him released.

Imagine Joseph's joy! He will be set free. No more prison. No more slavery. He can return to his father. He can go home.

He waits through the first day. Nothing. *Maybe tomorrow*, he says to himself. *Tomorrow will be celebration day.*

The next day passes. Again, nothing. He tells himself it is just some red tape. He thinks perhaps the butler is just waiting to make sure his timing is right.

Days turn into weeks, then months, and still Joseph sits, rotting in prison.

Eventually it becomes clear: The butler forgot. He has his own life. People tend to be obsessed with their own well-being. For two years, nearly as long as it took Lewis and Clark to cross a continent, Joseph sat alone. I wonder how often he thought this might be the end of his story.

But of course, it was not the end. God was not finished yet. Joseph would learn to see the deeper meaning of his suffering. As he would put it to his brothers, "Even though you intended to do harm to me, God intended it for good, in order to preserve a numerous people, as he is doing today." All of Joseph's best days—his rise in Egypt, his service to a nation, his impact as a leader, his reunion with his father, his reconciliation with his brothers—all lay on the other side of the Rockies. And that is because ultimately his story was a part of God's story.

Joseph's story reminds me of another story about a young man who was disappointed in the way his life turned out. *It's a Wonderful Life*, a staple for the Christmas season, is the story of a young man, George Bailey, who, like Joseph, was also a dreamer. He was going to travel the world, do great things, make his father proud. But none of these dreams was realized. He ended up trapped in a small town with a two-bit savings and loan company, wondering whether his life was worth anything. He, too, saw the wind.

I read recently that this movie is now much more popular than it was when it first came out. In 1946 its box-office performance was a bit of a disappointment. The writer of the article suggested that one reason for its resurgence is that it resonates with so many disappointed baby boomers who feel, like George Bailey, that life did not turn out the way they planned. They want to know that they matter, that what they have done is worthwhile after all. They want reassurance that when all is said and done, their overriding feeling will not be disappointment.

Dallas Willard writes,

> I meet many faithful Christians who, in spite of their faith, are deeply disappointed in how their lives have turned out. Sometimes it is simply a matter of how they experience aging, which they take to mean they no longer *have* a future. But often, due to circumstances or wrongful decisions and actions by others, what they had hoped to accomplish in life they did not. They painfully puzzle over what they may have done wrong, or whether God has really been with them.

Much of the distress of these good people comes from a failure to realize that their lives lie before them. Because they are coming to the end of their present lives, life "in the flesh" is of little significance. What is of significance is the kind of people they have become. Circumstances and other people are not in control of an individual's character or of the life that lies endlessly before us in the kingdom of God. Not jealous brothers or foolish fathers, not Potiphar or his wife, not forgetful butlers or proud pharaohs. There is a life that lies endlessly before us in the kingdom of God. And it's a wonderful life.

This is not always easy to believe. Sometimes it seems that bad news will get the last word. So perhaps it was not a surprise that in the greatest story of all, when God eventually sent one more dreamer, he ended up being another young man for whom things did not seem to turn out the way he had planned. He, too, wore a robe, a scarlet robe—the colorful indication of status. But it was given in mockery, and he, too, found his robe taken from him by those who intended to kill him.

Crowds mocked him, friends abandoned him, Peter denied him, Judas betrayed him, soldiers crucified him, and his body was laid in a tomb—one more dreamer, one more young man whose life turned out to be a disappointment.

Until ... on the third day ... he woke up feeling good. Ultimate resiliency.

On the third day, bad news lost for all time.

Ever since that third day, whatever bad news may enter your life has no power to separate you from God. For the story of this world is a good good news/bad news story.

Just wait until you reach the other side of the Rockies.

GETTING OUT OF THE BOAT

1. What role have problems played in your growth in the past?
2. What problem brings you the biggest concern these days—what's your "Rocky Mountain"? What is it exactly that you're afraid might happen as a result of this problem?
3. How would you describe your "resiliency factor"? How would you like it to grow?
4. How, with regard to a particular problem, could you move from passivity to exercising control and initiative?
5. In times of problems and stress, where do you find yourself most vulnerable to temptation?
6. If God were to speak to you in the area of your greatest current problem, what do you think he might say?

But when the disciples saw him walking on the sea, they were terrified, saying, "It is a ghost!" And they cried out in fear. But immediately Jesus spoke to them and said, "Take heart, it is I; do not be afraid."

Peter answered him, "Lord, if it is you, command me to come to you on the water." He said, "Come." So Peter got out of the boat, started walking on the water, and came toward Jesus. But when he noticed the strong wind, he became frightened, and beginning to sink, he cried out, "Lord, save me!"

Matthew 14:26–30

Crying Out in Fear

Nothing is so much to be feared as fear.

Henry David Thoreau

What would you guess is the most common command in Scripture?

It is not for us to be more loving. That may be the core to God's desire for human life, but that is not his most frequent instruction.

Writers about spiritual life often speak of pride as being at the root of human fallenness, but the Bible's most frequent imperative does not have to do with avoiding pride or gaining humility.

It is not a command to guard sexual purity or to walk with integrity, important as those qualities are.

The single command in Scripture that occurs more often than any other—God's most frequently repeated instruction—is formulated in two words:

Fear not.

Do not be afraid. Be strong and courageous. You can trust me. Fear not.

Why does God command us not to fear?

Fear does not seem like the most serious vice in the world. It never made the list of the Seven Deadly Sins. No one ever receives church discipline for being afraid. So why does God tell human beings to stop being afraid more often than he tells them anything else?

My hunch is that the reason God says "Fear not" so much is *not* that he wants us to be spared emotional discomfort. In fact, usually he says it to get people to do something that is going to lead them into greater fear anyway.

I think God says "fear not" so often because fear is the number one reason human beings are tempted to avoid doing what God asks them to do.

Fear is the number one reason why people refuse to get out of the boat. So we need this command all the time. Lloyd Ogilvie notes there are 366 "fear not" verses in the Bible—one for every day of the year, including one for leap year!

A Parable of Courage

A two-year-old girl stands by the side of a pool. "Jump!" her father says, with open arms. "Don't be afraid. You can trust me. I won't let you fall. Jump!"

She is, in that moment, a bundle of inner conflict. On the one hand, everything inside her is screaming to stay put. The water is deep, cold, and dangerous. She has never done this before. She can't swim. What if something were to go wrong? Bad things could happen. After all, it is *her* little body at stake here.

On the other hand, that is her daddy in the water. He is bigger and stronger than she is and has been relatively trustworthy up to this point for the past two years. He seems to be quite confident about the outcome.

The battle is between fear and trust.

Trust says, *Jump!*

Fear says, *No!*

She cannot stand on the side of the pool forever. Eventually she comes to the moment of decision. She is more than just her fears—or her confidence, for that matter. Inside is a tiny spark of *will*, and with that little spark she determines her destiny. She will jump, or she will back away.

Whichever way this little girl chooses will lead to significant consequences.

If she chooses to jump, she will become a little more confident of her father's ability to catch her. She will become more likely to take the leap next time. The water will hold less terror for her. Ultimately, she will come to see herself as the kind of person who will not be held back by fear.

On the other hand, if she decides not to jump, that will also have consequences. She will lose the opportunity to discover that her father can be trusted. She will be a little more inclined toward safety next time. She will perceive herself as the kind of person who does not respond bravely to challenges. She will work harder to make sure she avoids being faced with decisions involving fear in the future.

I want my children to have an appropriate fear of the water. When our girls were very small, I was playing in a pool with them at a hotel. We had warned Mallory (then two) not to get into deep water by herself or she could drown—though apparently we did not define this word well enough for her.

At one point when her older sister was jumping to me, I heard a splash behind me and turned to see that Mallory had stepped into the water and was completely submerged—for all of about half a second. I pulled her out immediately, and she began to cry out, "I drowned! Oh, I drowned!"

There is a place for fear. But I want trust to be stronger. I never want the *no* of fear to trump the *yes* of faith.

Fear makes two appearances in the story of Jesus walking on the water. First, the disciples are afraid because they do not understand that Jesus is with them in the storm. Dale Bruner writes,

> So Jesus says, "Courage! I AM! Fear not!" As we saw in chapter 1, Jesus is not just identifying himself ('It's me'); this is a revelation that the God "I AM" is in their midst. These are the words of Isaiah come to life:
>
> *Fear not,* for I have redeemed you;

I have called you by name, you are mine.
When you pass through the waters, I will be with you;
And through the rivers, they shall not overwhelm you....

For *I* AM the Lord your God,
the Holy One of Israel, your Savior ...,

and I love you.

A young disciple stood by the side of the boat. Jesus stood on the water. Jesus stretched out his hands and said, "Come."

Trust said, *Jump*.

Fear said, *No*.

Peter jumped. And for a while, everything went smoothly.

Then fear struck a second time. He saw the wind. And this led to the next phase—he became frightened. His response to the wind and the storm was to give in to fear. He lost his sense of confidence that Jesus was master of the situation. He did not just sink in the water, but sank in his own anxiety and worry.

> Fear disrupts faith and becomes the biggest obstacle to trusting and obeying God.

I believe the reason God says "fear not" so often is that fear will sink us faster than anything else. Fear disrupts faith and becomes the biggest obstacle to trusting and obeying God.

A middle-aged man feels called to switch careers, to do something bold for God—but fear holds him back.

A woman feels trapped in a marriage that is painful and abusive—but fear keeps her from acknowledging reality and seeking help.

A long-time Christian has a hard time loving God because she is afraid he will do bad things to her. When life goes too well for too long, she gets nervous. She is waiting for the other shoe to drop.

A young woman feels pressured by her parents to follow a course for her life that she does not want—but fear prevents her from speaking the truth.

A young man finds himself engaged to a woman with whom he is not in love—but everyone is expecting the marriage to take place. Fear keeps him from being aware of what truly lies within his heart and acting with authenticity.

Another man would love to search for intimacy and marriage, but fear keeps him from asking women out and entering into a serious relationship.

An elderly man is afraid of dying. He has never told anyone this—he is afraid of what others might think of him if they should find out.

A successful businessman risks financial security and market share every day. He never thinks of himself as fearful—he is a high-adventure, fearless paragon of courage. But he has not risked emotional intimacy or authentic self-disclosure since he was a child. He cannot risk losing control or displaying weakness—he is too afraid.

I have enormous admiration for people who genuinely struggle with fear, but in the moment of decision choose to jump. It is one thing when a Type T jumps. But for someone to whom risk does not come naturally to stand by the side of the boat and jump when God calls; for someone who wrestles with worry and doubt and yet still obeys, trembling but trusting—*that is true courage*. And any of us may do that. We may not all turn into hang-gliding, skydiving, bungee-jumping Type T personalities, but every one of us will face those moments when we must choose between trust and fear.

Trust and fear have been battling each other for the human heart—your heart—a long time now. Eventually one or the other will win.

Think about your life. Where is Jesus calling you to jump to him with reckless abandon? What is keeping you in the boat? I suspect it is fear.

Let's spend some time looking at the anatomy of fear. What is it, and what is the cost of living in it?

What Is Fear?

At its simplest and most benign, fear is an internal warning cry that danger is nearby and we had better do something about it. It is designed to be what researchers call a "self-correcting mechanism"—to be unpleasant enough to motivate us to take action and remove ourselves from whatever is threatening us. It readies our body to flee, hide, or fight.

There is a large physiological component to fear. A friend of mine was once trying to prepare for an upcoming conversation with a very intimidating person. He was talking about this with his wife and told her, "You know, when I think about doing this, my palms get sweaty."

About an hour later, unable to think of anything else, he said, "You know, when I think about doing this, my mouth gets dry."

Her advice to him: "Why don't you just lick your palms?"

What was going on that would make his body react this way? Fear involves several things. First, your mind senses you are in danger. In fact, the word *fear* comes from the Old English word for danger. Science writer Rush Dozier speaks of a primitive fear process centered in the limbic system that can detect danger within a tenth of a second of initial perception—before conscious decision-making has a chance to kick in. Certain experiences like loud noises or seeing extreme heights seem to be hard-wired into us to produce fear from birth. Scientists speak of some fears as innate while others are learned. Comedian-qua-theologian Dave Barry puts it like this: "All of us are born with a set of instinctive fears: of falling, of the dark, of lobsters, of falling on lobsters in the dark, of speaking before a Rotary Club, and of the words: 'some assembly required.'"

The incredible speed of this process helps us react immediately to potential trouble, but it also means our initial responses have not been filtered yet by a slower process—what has been called the rational fear system. (This is why, for instance, people on roller coasters or in horror movies can be simultaneously terrified and laughing—the primitive fear system is screaming that we are in danger while the rational fear system tells us we are okay.)

When a fear response is triggered, our bodies go into action. Quick-energy hormones, like adrenaline, get pumped into muscles and the bloodstream. Blood drains from the skin's surface (which is what produces the paleness of fear) and gets diverted into large muscles, like the legs, for a quick getaway. Your heart pounds to enable your body to go into overdrive. The eyes widen and pupils expand to take in the maximum amount of information. Many of the body's other systems—for reproduction, digestion, and so on—shut down to mobilize us for action.

There is such a thing as good fear: the fear that keeps a child from touching a hot stove, the fear that keeps you from driving recklessly, the fear that keeps a man from dressing the way he really wants to—in bold plaid colors that express his true personality—because he is afraid of what his wife may say.

If fear only happened when it was truly needed—when you are about to be struck by a truck or chased by a homicidal maniac—it would be nothing to worry about. The problem is that for most of us, fear strikes when it is neither helpful nor wanted. It can get attached to what does not truly threaten us and can become paralyzing instead of motivating.

In some cases fear ceases to be sporadic and becomes habitual. When this happens, we become *worriers*. Worry is a special form of fear. The traditional distinction is that fear is caused by an *external* source while worry or anxiety is produced from the *inside*. Yet they produce the same physical responses. Worry is fear that has unpacked its bags and signed a long-term lease. Worry never moves out of its own accord—it has to be evicted. Unfortunately, the very gift of imagination that makes the human mind so glorious also increases its vulnerability to worry. Joseph LeDoux, a neuroscientist at New York University, sums it up this way: "A rat can't worry about the stock market crashing." But we can.

> The very gift of imagination that makes the human mind so glorious also increases its vulnerability to worry.

We need to take the physical aspect of fear seriously. It is a natural part of being human. An article in the *New York Times Magazine* cited research that indicates some people have a strong predisposition toward fear and anxiety that is apparently genetic. They have even located the gene: the slc6a4 gene on chromosome 17q12. People who have a short version of this gene are more likely to worry than people who have a long version of it.

Now that you know this—are you worried you might have the short version?

This is one reason why it may be critical for a person to consult a doctor or psychiatrist to see if there is a physiological problem for constant anxiety. For example, certain forms of rumination or obsessive worries are associated with problems in a part of the brain called the cingulate cortex. Medications that help to keep cells in this area from over-firing are not a substitute for faith, just a reflection of the fact that we really are physical as well as spiritual beings.

For the most part, the number of commands in the Bible suggests that fear generally plays a destructive role in the lives of men and women. Fear, as you and I usually experience and handle it, is not a good thing.

Over and over in the Bible, it is *fear* that threatens to keep people from trusting and obeying God.

When that little girl stands by the side of the pool, she is usually well aware of the price she might pay by jumping in. It will be cold and scary, and (she's most afraid) she might die.

But she—and you and I—are often less aware that there is a price to be paid for refusing to jump. To live in chronic fear extracts the highest cost of all. Susan Jeffers puts it like this: "Pushing through the fear is less frightening than living with the underlying fear that comes from a feeling of helplessness." So let's consider the high cost of living in a mindset of fear.

Loss of Self-Esteem

The American Psychological Association published a book a few years ago that summarized all the research that has been done in recent years on self-esteem. They looked at a basic paradox: Why are there so many people lacking self-esteem who have many reasons to have high self-esteem? They accomplish many things—they are gifted, attractive, and well-liked—yet struggle with self-esteem. Even people who have accomplished a great deal and are apparently successful are often prone to feelings of self-doubt and inadequacy. Not only that, many people who receive much affirmation and admiration from significant others *tend to disbelieve it* and wrestle with self-esteem all the same.

All research suggests that self-esteem largely boils down to one issue: When you face a difficult situation, do you approach it, take action, and face it head on, or do you avoid it, wimp out, and run and hide?

If you take action, you get a surge of delight, even if things do not turn out perfectly. *I did a hard thing. I took on a challenge.* You grow.

When you avoid facing up to a threatening situation, even if things end up turning out all right, inside you say, *But the truth is, I wimped out. I didn't do the hard thing. I took the easy way out.*

Avoidance kills an inner sense of confidence and esteem. This is why praise from others, even when it is sincere, often does not help much. Avoiders become experts at "impression management"—pretending to be what they think will be acceptable to others. But even when we are successful at managing others' impressions of us and eliciting praise, inside we discount it: *If you only saw the truth about me, you wouldn't admire me. You're just admiring what I want you to see in me.* But when you take on a challenge, it builds the core of who you are, even if you don't perform flawlessly.

> When you take on a challenge, it builds the core of who you are, even if you don't perform flawlessly.

Recently I was on a cross-country flight with three friends who work at my church. The plane was packed, so we could not sit together. One of us threw out a challenge: "Let's see who can have the most significant spiritual conversation with a stranger on the way home." (I work at a high-challenge church.) Some people I know seem to convert fellow airline passengers on a regular basis, but I must fly the wrong airline, because that is certainly not my normal experience.

The challenge was presented. Now it was up to me to embrace or avoid it.

I sat down and met the man on my left. He was a businessman, hard at work on his laptop and wearing one of the most beautiful suits I have ever seen. He looked like an ad for whatever store ranks above Nordstrom's.

This is good, I thought, *because he probably has an expensive pen that I can ask to borrow to draw an illustration of the gospel, and he'll have to pay attention.*

It was not an ideal setting for conversation. The whole plane was testy because it was so crowded and because we were running late.

I greeted him over dinner and was working up to turning the conversation in a spiritual direction. However, I was having a problem getting the salad dressing to come out of its pouch. I applied tremendous pressure, and suddenly the whole thing traveled in one tremendous blob and covered his suit.

It was not a little dab. His pants looked like the skin of a Jersey cow.

It took the flight attendant and me twenty-five minutes to convince him that club soda could get the stain out.

He was in the washroom for thirty minutes.

Now I *really* wanted to go into avoidance mode. I kept wondering, *Where do I go from here?* The thought that kept coming to me was, *Club soda could get out the stain in your suit; what's going to get out the stain in your soul?* But I wasn't sure that approach would be effective.

We talked anyway, and it turned out he was already a Christian, and in fact he knew something about Willow Creek Church.

"So you work there?" he asked.

"Yes," I said. "My name is Bill Hybels."

Actually, I told him my real name, and we ended up having a significant conversation about spiritual life. But what I noted as I got off the plane was a sense of satisfaction in having embraced the challenge. I had not done it smoothly—not by a long shot. But there is something about embracing a challenge that is very important for inner well-being.

Mark it down: When you are in a situation that creates fear, but you face it head-on, you will feel a rush of satisfaction in knowing you displayed courage. Why don't you conduct your own experiment of trust this week? Sometime when you are tempted to avoid, hold your ground and press forward instead:

Stand up to a bully who is mistreating others (or you) at work. Wade feet first into a task that you have been putting off because you have feared it would be difficult or unpleasant. Express your true opinion when you are talking to a person you would normally try to placate or impress. Take responsibility for a tough decision you have been putting off. Make a phone call you have been trying to evade. Acknowledge to God in prayer a sin or character flaw you have been trying to hide. Ask for help in changing and tell another person about this.

When you do this, you will get a little stronger inside.

But when you wimp out by refusing to take the difficult step or saying the hard word—you die a little. And if that becomes a pattern, over time you come to see yourself as someone who cannot cope with life's greatest challenges. Where there ought to be an inner core of strength and resolve, you will experience fear and anxiety instead. You will learn to live in fear and avoidance.

And even if things turn out well externally and people are impressed with your life, you will be incurring an internal debt that you will pay off the rest of your life.

Loss of Destiny

If you live in fear, you will never experience the potential that God has placed in you.

As we have seen, growth always involves risk, and risk always involves fear.

I had lunch recently with a friend who is clearly being called by God to do some tremendous things in life. He is an enormously gifted person—a talented artist and a terrific writer. Yet he is in a job that is killing him. It doesn't call on his greatest abilities, and he has no passion for it. He is just punching the time clock. Why does he stay in it?

Fear. More specifically, the fear of failure. What if he tries something new, and it does not go well? What if he can't make enough money? What if people think he is foolish? What if he turns out not to be as gifted as he thought?

In an odd way, he is also afraid of success. If he succeeds, people may expect more from him. The stakes may go up. His sense of pressure may rise even higher. Sometimes people are even more frightened of succeeding than they are of failing.

> Sometimes people are even more frightened of succeeding than they are of failing.

So, until he can get some ironclad guarantee that everything will work out exactly right, until all risk is removed, he will stay where he is—and stagnate.

Eventually, if this pattern does not change, it will come time for my friend to retire, and he will be relieved to quit and will try to be as comfortable as he can for the remaining years of his life.

And he will never have done what God created him to do, never have become what God created him to be. Fear will cost him his destiny—and that is too high a price to pay.

Loss of Joy

Have you ever met a deeply joyful, chronically worried person? Fear destroys joy. Live in it, and you will know the pain of constant, chronic, low-grade anxiety. Transcend it, and you will know delight.

Another friend of mine is up to his neck in a very difficult challenge. The stakes—relationally, emotionally, and spiritually—are extremely high. "I have never been so far out on a limb with God," he told me. "I keep telling the other people involved, 'Trust him! God really will work!' And now all I can think is—*he better!*" I looked at my friend and saw in his face all the marks of someone courageously seeking to trust and obey—excitement, anticipation, suspense, prayer, a deep sense of dependence, significant activity, being stretched to the capacity of his abilities. I realized that he is having the time of his life. This is simply life at its best. He is out of the boat. Trusting in the face of fear and challenge produces joy.

On the other hand, giving in to fear is a joy-killer. According to current research, most worriers tend to have high-capacity imaginations. They usually carry above-average IQs. They are often people with much creative potential.

But their imaginations run toward the negative. They tend to catastrophize:

—What if bad things happen?
—What if I get in an accident and wreck the car?
—What if I lose my wallet?
—What if I preach a poor sermon?

All these things are contingent, set in the future, and may never happen at all! In fact, most of them won't.

But when I live with a fear-filled perspective, I give such things power to rob me of life *now!*

A healthy sense of perspective allows us to assign these events a realistic assessment that helps us get on with life.

—What if you wreck your car? *You can get a new one.*
—What if you lose your wallet? *You can get a new one.*
—What if the teaching pastor gives a poor sermon? *You can send him to Hawaii for a sabbatical.*

But when you live in fear, the power of the "what if" becomes overwhelming, and you will go through life without joy. Joy and fear are fundamentally incompatible.

Loss of Authentic Intimacy

Fear and hiding go together like adolescence and hormones. The very first recorded instance of fear reflects this: *Where were you, Adam?*

I heard you in the garden, And I was afraid, because I was naked, so I hid.

And we have been hiding ever since—behind smiles we don't really feel, behind agreeable words we don't really believe, mostly behind the things we truly feel and believe but refuse to say.

When I was growing up, my parents would sometimes have my brother, sister, and me play "the quiet game." I imagine you know the rules: Whoever could be the quietest the longest wins. It is a popular game with parents.

One day we were playing—for hours, we kids being unusually good at this game—when the thought suddenly occurred to me: *I don't have to play the quiet game.*

—I don't have to play the quiet game because ... *I don't really think my parents would punish me for talking.*
—I don't have to play the quiet game because ... *even if they did, no punishment could be worse than having to sit here in silence mile after mile after mile.*
—I don't have to play the quiet game because ... *I'm seventeen years old now, and this is getting ridiculous.*

I hate to say it, but sometimes—for altogether different reasons these days—I still play the quiet game. All too often I hold back from saying what I truly think or feel because of fear. I am afraid of what someone might think of me; or I am afraid of the pain in the conflict that might emerge; or I am afraid that I will have to spend more energy cleaning up the relational mess that will emerge than I really want to spend.

You play the quiet game when you pretend something does not bother you when it really does; or when you pretend to agree with someone when you really don't; or when you act as if you don't care, but you really do.

People in churches are often good at playing the quiet game in the name of peace, but it is not peace built on truth. In fact, it is not real peace at all; it is just the absence of conflict made possible by hiding.

I know of couples who have played the quiet game with each other for years. They play it to avoid arguments—but they also avoid intimacy.

I know employees who play the quiet game at work. They play it in order to avoid making waves or rocking the boat—but they spend years in resentment and frustration.

I know Christians who play the quiet game with unchurched neighbors and friends. They may avoid embarrassment or rejection—but they lose the chance to fearlessly share their faith and offer spiritual life to people far from God.

I wonder whom you might be playing the quiet game with: a boss? a spouse? an assertive relative? a strong-willed child? an opinionated coworker? an intimidating authority figure?

Fear always lies behind the quiet game.

Loss of Availability to God

Fear whispers to us that God is not really big enough to take care of us. It tells us we are not really safe in his hands. It causes us to distort the way we think about him.

When I was seeing clients as an intern in graduate school, one of my clients had a phobia related to flying. She had gone through a traumatic experience on a plane as a little girl and had never quite recovered from it.

I had her go through a process called systematic desensitization, which involves learning to relax (it is physically impossible for the body to experience fear in a relaxed state) while having increasingly vivid mental pictures about flying, until eventually the person is able to fly. Because she was a Christian, we also spent some time talking about where God was in all this.

"Don't you know," I told her, "that he's with you everywhere? Some of Jesus' last words were, 'I am with you always.'"

"No," she laughed. "What he actually said was, 'Low—I am with you always.'"

There is no limit to his presence. There is no place where we can go, no activity we can engage in, where he is not watching over us. "When you pass through the waters, I will be with you."

But fear tries to convince us it is not so. Fear has created more practicing heretics than bad theology ever has, for it makes us live as though we serve a limited, finite, partially present, semi-competent God.

I think of a woman who was in a dating relationship with a man although she knew it was not right. There were serious, unresolved sinful patterns in his life. She knew what was at stake. But if she broke up—she might be alone. She didn't think she could handle that, so she married him. And she is more alone now than she was when she was single.

What kept her in a relationship she *knew* she should break free of? Fear.

She was afraid that God would not be adequate to protect her from unbearable loneliness.

And now she is headed for a mountain of regret. She wonders, "What if I had trusted him?"

You will never know God is trustworthy if you don't risk obeying him. When you come to the end of your life—all those "what ifs" become "might have beens."

What might have been if I had trusted God?

If you give in to a mindset of fear and find yourself one day, at the end of your life, filling your days in a comfortable chair in front of a television set, the thought will come: *What might have been? If I had trusted God—what might I have done? What might I have become?*

It is a price too high to pay.

Fear Gets Passed from Generation to Generation

Social science researchers say we are the most worried culture that has ever lived.

Life expectancy has more than doubled in the past century. We are able to cure more diseases than ever before. No group of human beings has ever been healthier, yet no group has ever been more worried about their health. We keep reading articles about how sick we are.

Journalist Bob Garfield tracked health articles in the *Washington Post, USA Today,* and the *New York Times* and discovered that, according to experts,

—59 million Americans have heart disease
—53 million suffer migraines
—25 million have osteoporosis
—16 million struggle with obesity
—3 million have cancer
—12 million have severe disorders such as brain injuries....

The results are that 543 million Americans are seriously sick—which is shocking in a country of 266 million people. As Garfield notes, "Either as a society we are doomed, or someone is seriously double-dipping."

Leonard Sweet writes,

The fear thing is dominating our need for security. Just look at our cars to see the security issue at work. First we install seat belts. Then we install shoulder belts. Then we build contraptions that put both together. Then we turn the shoulder harness into a boa constrictor that pins us to our seats and doesn't let us move. Then we install air bags. Pretty soon we'll be riding around inside a giant marshmallow."

The media frighten us because fear sells.

Government agencies are often set up so their continued funding depends on a public perception that they are protecting us from frightening risks.

In addition, many of us learned about fear in families. What did Mom say when you went out the door to school? It is the rare mom who says, Take risks today. Embrace danger. Look just one way when you cross street.

Usually maternal advice runs along the lines of Be careful. You could get hurt. Don't play with that stick—you could poke out someone's eye.

In all your life, have you ever known anybody who lost an eye playing with sticks? We're raised to be scared.

For parents this may be the worst part of all. Your hopes, dreams, and callings are impaired by distorted fears and worry. Thus, you will be limiting the hopes, dreams, and callings of your children. They will learn from you that the only way to go through life is with anxiety and fear.

> No group of human beings has ever been healthier, yet no group has ever been more worried about their health.

On the other hand, fear isn't the only thing that spreads. So does trust. Daring faith is contagious as well.

Sometime ago I took my then ten-year-old son parasailing. The man driving the boat said he could ascend to 400, 600, or 800 feet. "How high above the water do you want to fly?"

There was a pretty big price difference, so I wanted to steer him toward 400 feet.

Then my son commented on how the whole idea was a little scary. It struck me that when I was ten years old, being lifted 800 feet up in the air behind a speeding boat over a deep lake might make me swallow extra hard. And I wanted him to be free of fear. So we talked through his options.

He thought it over for a few minutes, and he finally decided, "I'm gonna go 800 feet up. I might be scared when I go up there at first. But I'm going to do it because the ride only lasts a few minutes. But once it's over, I'll have it forever."

I think if God had anything to say to you now, it might be this: *The ride only lasts a few minutes.* "As for mortals, their days are like grass; they flourish like a flower of the field; for the wind passes over it, and it is gone,*

133

*and its place knows it no more." In the vast eternal scheme of things, your
life is briefer than you could possibly imagine.*

> *But whatever you do in faith,*
> *Every time you trust me,*
> *Whenever you act in risky obedience and jump in response to my
invitation—*
> *That you will have forever.*
> *Go ahead and jump.*

GETTING OUT OF THE BOAT

1. On a "Fear Management Scale" of 1–10, where would you rate
   yourself between 1 ("I'm often paralyzed by fear") and 10 ("I
   almost never let fear stop me")?
2. What lessons did you learn about fear as you were growing up? Was
   your family more fearless or fearful?
3. What is your greatest fear?
4. Which of the "high costs of fear" do you feel most keenly these
   days?
5. What is one step you can take today to "feel the fear and do it
   anyway"?

So Peter got out of the boat, started walking on the water, and came toward Jesus. But when he noticed the strong wind, he became frightened, and beginning to sink, he cried out, "Lord, save me!" Jesus immediately reached out his hand and caught him, saying to him, "You of little faith, why did you doubt?"

Matthew 14:29–31

That Sinking Feeling

He who has never failed somewhere, that man cannot be great. Failure is the test of greatness.

Herman Melville

Our drive for mastery and growth seems to start in the crib. When one of our daughters (whose earliest nickname was "May-May) was very small, her favorite sentence consisted of the words, "May-May do it by herself." She said it whenever people tried to offer her unwanted help. It is a safe bet that she has said it thousands of times. She wanted to be in the arena. She would rather have known the exhilaration of trying even if it ended in defeat than to have a guaranteed outcome at the expense of passivity and adventure.

She would try to walk and would crash into things, and then we would want to help. She would wave us away: *May-May do it by herself.*

When she was not much older, she would get on her little bike and crash into things, and we would want to help: *May-May do it by herself.*

It makes me a little nervous because very soon May-May is goir to be old enough to drive a car, and since we have a pattern go' know what she's going to say.

When we are young, failure does not seem to affect us much. No one-year-old stumbles when he tries to walk, then says to himself, *Well, that was stupid and clumsy of me! I guess I wasn't cut out to be a walker. I sure don't want anybody else to watch me fall. I'd rather settle for crawling the rest of my life than put myself through that experience again.*

Children are perfectly content to put up with unsteadiness and falling on the way to walking. That is why we call them toddlers. It is all they are capable of doing. They *expect* to toddle.

But as we grow older, we seem to grow more afraid of falling. We would rather avoid going down than learn to walk.

Peter was a water-toddler. His steps, like his faith, were uncertain. He was willing to risk failure for the adventure of trusting Christ more fully. And Jesus is not about to treat Peter's failure as grounds for dismissal. He takes Peter's faith seriously—Peter has some things to learn—but he starts by rescuing him. As Dale Bruner notes, Jesus does scold Peter; he diagnoses the area of trouble. But fortunately, "Jesus saves before he scolds." Both the saving *and* the scolding are evidences of Jesus' love for Peter.

I believe this is one of the most important questions in life: *Why is it that for some people failure is energizing, while for others failure is paralyzing?*

All of us experience failure, and no one likes it. But for some people it becomes a kind of goad to push on to new learning, deeper persistence, more vigorous commitment, more courageous hearts. For others failure produces utter defeat—a sense of discouragement, a loss of hope, a desire to hide, a secret resolve to never again get out of the boat.

People's perceptions of and responses to failure make an enormous difference in their lives—more than IQ, physical attractiveness, charm, and financial assets put together. Those who can learn from it, retaining a deep sense of their own value and marshaling the motivation to try again, become masters of failure management. Psychologist Daniel Goleman cites a number of studies that identify the very top performers in fields from athletics to music. What sets them apart, he notes, is the doggedness that stems from certain "emotional traits—enthusiasm and persistence in the face of setbacks—above all else."

To consider this trait, let's look at a time of failure in the life of one of the most adventurous men who ever lived—King David.

The Scriptures relate that for a long time David experienced a glittering string of successes. He was anointed by Samuel to be king of Israel. As a boy he defeated Israel's most formidable enemy—Goliath. King Saul chose him as a warrior and musician. The army loved him, the people wrote songs about him: "Saul has killed his thousands, David his ten thousands."

David knew what it was to walk on water. He trusted God, and for a long time everything he touched turned to gold. He was on his way to the palace.

Then a strange thing happened. One by one all those wonderful things he had been given were stripped away. David lost his job. He had been promoted from shepherd to court musician to warrior—the most successful officer in the army. But now Saul was jealous. He started chucking spears, and David was out of a job. With it, David lost his income and his security. He would never serve in Saul's army again.

Next, he lost his wife. He had married Saul's daughter, Michal, but Saul sent soldiers to kill David. Michal helped him escape, but she was taken back by Saul and ended up marrying someone else. (David later got her back, as we read in 2 Samuel 3—they had some strange marriage customs in those days!).

So David fled to Ramah, where Samuel, his spiritual mentor, lived. Samuel was the one who anointed David when he was young. Samuel was the one who assured David of God's presence in his life. Samuel was the one through whom God spoke to David. Samuel, David knew, would be a safe person.

But Saul heard where David went and sent soldiers after him. David had to make another escape, and Samuel could not go with him—he was an old man. Indeed, Samuel died not long afterward.

Next, David ran to his best friend, Jonathan, who had stood up to his father, Saul, and risked his life for David. But Jonathan would not leave the court. He could not—or would not—raise the sword against his own father. So once more David was on his own and had to run for his life.

His job and marriage had ended in failure, his mentor had died, his best friend was out of his life. Then it got worse.

David fled his home and ran to Gath, hometown of the late giant Goliath. David had nowhere to go but to the Philistines, his mortal enemies. This move did not turn out to be any more successful than the others. David was

> very much afraid of King Achish of Gath. So he changed his behavior before them; he pretended to be mad when in their presence. He scratched marks on the doors of the gate, and let his spittle run down his beard. Achish said to his servants, "Look, you see the man is mad; why then have you brought him to me? Do I lack madmen, that you have brought this fellow to play the madman in my presence? Shall this fellow come into my house?"

Having failed to find a refuge in Gath, David ran once more. "David left [Gath] and escaped to the cave of Adullam."

The Cave Named Failure

Whereas once David had wealth, power, fame, friends, security, and what he thought was a guaranteed future, now he was running for his life and living in a cave.

It is called the cave of Adullam, but we might think of it as the cave named Failure. The cave is where you end up when your props, supports, and crutches get stripped away. The cave is where you find yourself when you thought you were going to do great things, have a great family, or boldly go where no one had gone before, and it becomes clear that things will not work out as you dreamed. Perhaps you are in the cave because of foolish choices. Perhaps it is a result of circumstances you could not even control. Most likely it is a combination of the two.

Perhaps you are in the cave right now—

Maybe it is because you have lost your job, or you are under financial pressure. Maybe it is because your dreams about family life have been shattered. Maybe you have lost a mentor or a best friend; there was a relationship you counted on, and now it is gone. Maybe it involves a physical condition—you have lost your health. Or you may simply find yourself alone.

For whatever reason, you are in the cave.

If you are not in the cave right now, wait a while—you will be. Nobody plans on ending up in the cave, but sooner or later everybody logs some time there.

The hardest thing about being in the cave is that you begin to wonder whether God has lost track of you. Did he forget his promises? Does he remember where I am? Will I ever be anywhere but in the cave? Will I die in here?

There is one other thing you need to know. The cave is where God does some of his best work in molding and shaping human lives. Sometimes, when all the props and crutches in your life get stripped away and you find you have only God, you discover that God is enough. Sometimes, when your worst fears of inadequacy are confirmed and you discover that you really are out of your league, you experience the liberation of realizing that it is okay to be inadequate and that God wants his power to flow through your weakness.

Sometimes the cave is where you meet God, for God does some of his best work in caves.

David knew about failure. He spent about ten years of his life in the wilderness on the run. From a human perspective it looked as if God's promises to him would never come true.

He was not entirely alone. He did have some people come to him to form a little community. But they were not a very promising group. "Everyone who was in distress, and everyone who was in debt, and everyone who was discontented gathered to him; and he became captain over them." This was not the cream of the crop he had to work with; rather, they were bankrupt, agitated whiners. He and this motley crew established a kind of refugee community in a village called Ziklag. They had taken wives and started families, and periodically they would go raiding other villages.

One day they came home and discovered that their village was gone. Ziklag had been sacked, their wives and children carried off. We are told that David and the people with him raised their voices and wept "until they had no more strength to weep."

Have you ever wept like that? Wept until there were no more tears left inside you? Wept until your body was so exhausted from weeping that you didn't even have the energy to cry? David understood tears like that.

That sounds bad enough, but for David things could still get worse. His men's grief turned to anger—and their anger was turned toward David. (Remember—these were not exactly Dale Carnegie grads to begin with.) "David was in great danger; for the people spoke of stoning him, because all the people were bitter in spirit for their sons and daughters."

Then comes one of the great statements in Scripture: "But David strengthened himself in the LORD his God."

This is a great secret of spiritual life. When every other resource was gone, when every prop was kicked out from under him and every crutch taken away, when he reached the point of utter failure, David encouraged himself in the Lord.

> When he reached the point of utter failure, David encouraged himself in the Lord.

How does this happen? How do people living in the cave of failure find the strength to venture out? Let's consider what is involved in the art of receiving divine encouragement.

I believe that the starting point in dealing with failure is to honestly face and name our discouragement. This is where David starts. We read about this in Psalm 142, described in its superscription as "A Maskil of David. When he was in the cave." The psalm was associated with this era of David's life; it was the cry of his heart when he felt destroyed by failure. This is a psalm for cave dwellers.

> With my voice I cry to the LORD;
> with my voice I make supplication to the LORD.
> I pour out my complaint before him;
> I tell my trouble before him.

Are you able to complain? Have you discovered that it is in fact your spiritual gift? If you can complain, you can take this step. Old Testament scholars tell us there are different kinds of psalms. Some are called psalms of thanksgiving, some are enthronement psalms about the king, some are psalms of wisdom, and so on. But the single most

~? vent

popular category is called the (psalm of lament.) The most frequent psalm consists of somebody complaining to God.

And God is apparently not put off by this at all. God allows people to do this—in fact, he encourages it. This is what David does in the cave. He gets quiet enough before the Lord to get to the bottom of his pain and discouragement. He feels it in his gut.

However, many people never have the courage to do this. Instead, they seek to bury their discouragement deep down inside. They put on a stoic exterior. They force a few smiles, but in doing so they avoid experiencing the pain inside.

Failure in our day often carries with it shame—the shame not just of having experienced failure, but of _being_ a failure. And facing this feeling is one of the hardest things a human being can do.

I have visited the churchyard where Shakespeare is buried in Stratford-upon-Avon. His body was put eighteen feet underground instead of the usual six to make sure no one would dig it up again. I have come to realize that I sometimes do that with my own sense of failure. I run for a class office at school, and lose. It tears at my need to have an image of a popular class leader; I feel low-grade embarrassment; I wish I had not run at all. But I don't talk about this with people. I do not even spend the time or effort to look deeply at it myself, to ask why it hurts, or what I might learn. I just want to put it eighteen feet under.

I apply for a position in college, but don't make it. I play in the finals of a tennis tournament that I have always dreamed of winning, against a player I know I can beat—and I lose. I reach for a cherished vocational goal, but fall short.

What I regret most as I look back on these experiences is not that I failed. Rather, I regret feeling the pain of failure so keenly that I backed away from owning it and learning from it, so I could not heal and move on. I wanted to bury it so deeply that no one would ever guess it was there—not even me. So I have needed to learn to pray the psalm of lament.

When I am honest about it and begin to explore beneath the surface, I discover that much of the pain of failure for me is not just that I have not achieved something—it is that other people might _think_ of me as failing.

One day a man named Elijah found himself in a cave. He had been by any definition an extremely successful prophet, taking on four hundred opponents and an evil king and offering faultless weather forecasts to boot. But the opposition of a single queen triggered something in him. Maybe he had been running on adrenaline too long; maybe his faith was too weak. At any rate, he was suddenly gripped with fear he could not manage; he was certain he had been a failure: "It is enough; now, O LORD, take away my life, for I am no better than my ancestors."

But God did not take away his life. God had a plan for Elijah to go out with a little more style later on. Perhaps God was not concerned that Elijah had to be all that much better than his ancestors. At any rate, God was very tender—he had an angel bake him a cake on hot stones (I'm tempted to say something about the origins of angel food cake) and direct Elijah to get some sleep. All in all, God treated Elijah the way you do a cranky toddler—have a snack, take a nap, and we'll talk when you're a little more composed. You'll toddle another day.

Elijah went up the mountain to the cave and was told that the Lord was about to pass by. (As we have already seen, this is the phrase that indicates an epiphany—a manifestation of God.) After a great wind, an earthquake, and fire came "a sound of sheer silence." And then came a still small voice, as God asked Elijah a wonderful question: "What are you doing here?" The best part of the question is that God did not say, "What are you doing *there?*" God was with Elijah in the cave.

I wonder whether Elijah was surprised by this. In times of great success it is not hard to believe that God is present. I suspect that when Elijah defied the prophets of Baal and saw fire from heaven consume offering and altar in response to a single prayer, he knew God was there. I suspect that when he foretold the end of the drought, when he revived the widow's child, when he outran the chariot, when he told off the king and got away with it, he knew God was with him.

But I think perhaps that the cave is the most wonderful place of all to find that you are loved by God. If you know—really know—that you are loved by God when you feel the weight of failure, then there is no place where you will be beyond the confines of his care.

One of the great gifts failure can give us is the recognition that we are loved and valued by God *precisely when we are in the cave of failure*.

It was in the cave that David cried out to God, "You are my refuge, my portion in the land of the living." As long as my sense of being valuable and significant is tied to my success, it will be a fragile thing. But when I come to know in the marrow of my bones that I am just as valued and loved by God when I have fallen flat on my face, *then* I am gripped by a love stronger than success *or* failure.

You can risk being fully honest with God for a very important reason: God is never a God of discouragement. When you have a discouraging spirit or train of thought in your mind, you can be sure it is not from God. He sometimes brings pain to his children—conviction over sin, or repentance over fallenness, or challenges that scare us, or visions of his holiness that overwhelm us. But God never brings discouragement. Always, his guidance leads to motivation and life.

Sometime ago I asked a spiritual mentor of mine, "How do you assess the well-being of your soul? How do you gauge your spiritual condition?"

My friend said that the first question he asks himself is this: *Am I growing more easily discouraged these days?* "Because," he told me, "if I'm walking closely with God, if I have the sense of God being with me, I find that problems lose their ability to damage my spirit."

Take Action

David's next step was to ask the priest to bring him the ephod—a sacred vestment worn originally by the high priest while ministering in the sanctuary—so he can inquire of the Lord what to do next. The ephod was a reminder of the presence of God. Scripture here is reminding us that David, like Peter when he got out of the boat, is seeking to discern what the Lord's will is. David, too, wants to distinguish faith from foolishness.

David received a very clear message from the ephod: "Pursue; for you shall surely overtake and shall surely rescue." So he took action, and in doing so, he rescued his community and reclaimed his leadership.

Taking action is very powerful. The reason many people become paralyzed in discouragement is because they fail to devote the time or energy to understand what was involved in the failure in the first place, and then they fail to take action toward change. They wait for some outside force or person to rescue them when God is calling them to action.

In any arena where you are concerned about failure, the single most destructive thing you can do is *nothing*. Psychologist David Burns writes about what he calls the cycle of lethargy: When I'm faced with a challenge and I do nothing, it leads to distorted thoughts—that I am helpless, hopeless, and beyond change. These in turn lead to destructive emotions—loss of energy and motivation, damaged self-esteem, feeling overwhelmed. The end result is self-defeating behavior—procrastination, avoidance, and escapism. These behaviors then reinforce negative thoughts, and the whole cycle spirals downward.

The good news is that God has made us in such a way that taking one single step of action can be extremely powerful in robbing failure of its power. For example, take marital failure. Psychologist Neil Warren says that lack of hope is what kills marriage more than anything else. When hope dies, the motivation to change dies, and you quit trying. At that point, the death of the marriage is just a matter of time.

Warren recommends focusing on one area in your marriage where you are discouraged and aiming for only a 10 percent improvement in twelve months. If you can improve 10 percent (which is not a huge goal), you will have gained something much more important: hope.

Many couples come to him discouraged about their sexual relationship. Warren says it is there where expectations often disconnect. Many husbands want sex in the morning; many wives want sex in ... June. If a couple can experience any noticeable improvement as a result of their efforts, they learn that effort pays off. They are not powerless victims. Hope gets born—and hope always trumps discouragement.

The alternative to taking action is passivity and resignation. One of Winnie the Pooh's friends is a gloomy donkey named Eeyore, who adopts this approach to life. Ward off the pain of discouragement by renouncing hope. This course must have been tempting to David at some points: *I guess I'll just live in a cave for the rest of my life. I'll just let Saul be king, then. I'm not surprised things didn't work out.*

But you can know that is not God's will for your life. God is *never* a God of discouragement! Failure can be a tremendous motivator. When I allow myself to experience the pain of failure, it can drive me to make the changes that will lead to new learning.

Sometimes failure simply involves our failure to persist in trying when we should continue. Gilbert Brim reminds us that five of the best-selling books of the twentieth century were each rejected by more than a dozen publishers before finally being accepted: Richard Hooker's *M*A*S*H** was rejected by twenty-one publishers; Thor Heyerdahl's *Kon-Tiki,* twenty; *Jonathan Livingston Seagull* by Richard Bach, eighteen (in large part because publishers mistook it as a book for children); Patrick Dennis's *Auntie Mame,* seventeen; and the record setter for this group, Dr. Seuss's first book, *And to Think That I Saw It on Mulberry Street*—an incredible twenty-three rejections.

Parker Palmer writes about a time in his life when he experienced the cave of deep depression. His action step was to experience a program called Outward Bound.

> I chose the weeklong course at Hurricane Island, off the coast of Maine. I should have known from that name what was in store for me; next time I will sign up at Happy Gardens or Pleasant Valley....
>
> In the middle of the week I faced the challenge I feared most. One of our instructors backed me up to the edge of a cliff 110 feet above solid ground. He tied a very thin rope to my waist—a rope that looked ill-kept to me and seemed to be starting to unravel—and told me to start rappelling down that cliff.
>
> "Do what?" I asked.
>
> "Just go!" the instructor explained, in typical Outward Bound fashion. So I went—and immediately slammed into a ledge, some four feet down from the edge of the cliff, with bone-jarring, brain-jarring force.
>
> The instructor looked down at me: "I don't think you've quite got it."
>
> "Right," said I, being in no position to disagree. "So what am I supposed to do?"
>
> "The only way to do this," he said, "is to lean back as far as you can. You have to get your body at right angles to the cliff so that your weight will be on your feet. It's counterintuitive, but it's the only way it works." I knew that he was

wrong, of course. I knew that the trick was to hug the mountain, to stay as close to the rock as I could. So I tried again, my way—and slammed into the next ledge, another four feet down.

"You still don't have it," the instructor said helpfully.

"OK," I said, "tell me again what I am supposed to do."

"Lean way back," he said, "and take the next step." The next step was a very big one, but I took it—and, wonder of wonders, it worked. I leaned back into empty space, my eyes fixed on the heavens in prayer, made tiny, tiny moves with my feet, and started descending down the rock face, gaining confidence with every step.

I was about halfway down when the second instructor called up from below, "Parker, I think you'd better stop and see what's just below your feet." I lowered my eyes very slowly and saw that I was approaching a deep hole in the face of the rock.

To get down, I would have to get around that hole, which meant I could not maintain the straight line of descent I had started to get comfortable with. I would need to change course and swing myself around that hole. I knew for a certainty that attempting to do so would lead directly to my death—so I froze, paralyzed with fear.

The second instructor let me hang there, trembling, in silence, for what seemed like a very long time. Finally, she shouted up these helpful words: "Parker, is anything wrong?"

To this day, I do not know where my words came from, though I have twelve witnesses to the fact that I spoke them. In a high, squeaky voice, I said, "I don't want to talk about it."

"Then," said the second instructor, "it's time that you learned the motto of Outward Bound."

Oh keen, I thought. I'm about to die, and she's going to give me a motto!

But then she shouted ten words that I hope never to forget, words whose impact and meaning I can still feel: "If you can't get out of it, get into it!"

This is your life, and these are *your* failures. No helicopter is going to come to whisk you away. No genie will pop out of a bottle to rescue you. No magic eraser will make things disappear.

This is your life. You can't get out of it. So get into it. Take one step toward trusting God in an area where you feel failure:

—Make a phone call to confront a situation that you've been avoiding

—Open a book to begin studying for a project you have been putting off because it feels overwhelming

—Write one letter to begin pursuing a job that would be a dream to you

—Take one class to try to acquire a new skill that will lead to significant growth in your life.

One small step of action is often worth a hundred internal pep talks. But you must remember one thing: You must be willing to fail.

In the movie *Chariots of Fire*, English runner Harold Abrams runs against the Scottish champion Eric Liddell and loses for the first time in his life. The pain of failure is so great he decides he cannot race again.

His girlfriend, Cybil, says, "Harold, this is absolutely ridiculous. It's a race you've lost, not a relative. Nobody's dead."

Harold moans, "I've lost."

"I know. I was there. I remember watching you; it was marvelous. *You* were marvelous. He was more marvelous, that's all. On that day the best man won.... He was ahead, there was nothing you could have done. He won fair and square."

"Well, that's that," Abrams says.

"If you can't take a beating, perhaps it's for the best."

"I don't run to take beatings—I run to win!" Harold shouts. "If I can't win, I won't run."

Cybil pauses, and then says to him firmly, *"If you don't run, you can't win."*

To run the best race you can, to give it everything that is in you, and win—that is glorious. To run the race, to give your best and lose—that's painful. But it is not failure. *Failure is refusing to run the race at all.*

Failure as Teacher

Parker Palmer's story indicates another important part of failure management—taking the time and having the courage to learn from failure.

A book called *Art and Fear* shows how indispensably failure is tied to learning. A ceramics teacher divided his class into two groups. One group would be graded solely on quantity of work—fifty pounds of pottery would be an "A," forty would be a "B," and so on. The other group would be graded on quality. Students in that group had to produce only one pot—but it had better be good.

Amazingly, all the highest quality pots were turned out by the quantity group. It seems that while the quantity group kept churning out pots, they were continually learning from their disasters and growing as artists. The quality group sat around theorizing about perfection and worrying about it—but they never actually got any better. Apparently—at least when it comes to pottery—trying and failing, learning from failure, and trying again works a lot better than waiting for perfection. No pot, no matter how misshapen, is really a failure. Each is just another step on the road to an "A." It is a road littered with imperfect pots. But there is no other road.

> Trying and failing, learning from failure, and trying again works a lot better than waiting for perfection.

Peter was in the quantity group. His water-walking was not a piece of perfection. But after it was done, Jesus helped him learn about his failure ("You of little faith, why did you doubt?"). His faith wasn't "A" material yet. But it was at least a little stronger than that of the eleven disciples sitting in the quality group. Next time out, Peter's faith would be a little stronger.

The cave is the place where we can learn from failure and follow God's plans. One day Saul brought three thousand soldiers with him to search for David. "He came to the sheepfolds beside the road, where there was a cave; and Saul went in to relieve himself." (The writer is telling us a little more here than we want to know, but he wants us to understand Saul's vulnerability at that moment.) David and his men were at the back of the same cave. His men told David, in so many words, "This must be the day the Lord spoke of! He's delivered Saul into your hands. God doesn't want you unhappy and miserable in this cave. You can be king. One thrust of the sword and all your dreams come true."

It must have been so tempting for David to think, *I could get out of the cave now. No more hiding. No more failure. I could be king.*

But he would not do it. In the cave David discovered that, more than he wanted to be king, he wanted to belong to God. He would rather please God and live in a cave than displease God and sit on the throne.

In the long run, being king—achieving outward success—was not a big enough dream for David. He had a better dream—to please God.

Contrast what David learned with Willy Loman. Willy Loman is the central character in Arthur Miller's *Death of a Salesman*, one of the greatest plays about failure and broken dreams ever written. Willy has spent his life chasing the dream of being an irresistibly successful salesman. So he lives in denial and vacillates between the illusion that tomorrow will bring the great success and moments of despair when he feels utterly worthless. He tortures himself with the belief that if he were just persistent enough or self-confident enough, he would be a success, and that success would be the fulfillment of his dreams.

If he had had the courage to fully face the pain of his sense of failure, if he could have sat still for a time with the reality of his emptiness, Willy might have perceived that he was pursuing the wrong dream and trying to be someone he was not. In the end, he commits suicide. His son, Biff, comes to see the truth about his dad:

> There were a lot of nice days. When he'd come home from a trip; or on Sundays, making the stoop; finishing the cellar; putting on the new porch.... You know something, Charley, there's more of him in that front stoop than in all the sales he ever made.... He had the wrong dreams. All, all wrong.... He never knew who he was.

The cave of failure offers a precious chance to learn. But we must be willing to ask courageous questions:

—Am I chasing the right dream?

—Is what I'm pursuing consistent with God's calling on my life?

—Am I operating out of what God made me to do, or out of my own needs for appearing important and significant?

—Am I willing to remain in the cave if it means being true to God?

Finding Ultimate Refuge

In the cave David says to God, "You are my refuge." Of course, we know the rest of the story. We know that David will not die in the cave. We know there is a crown ahead.

But David does not. For all he knows, this cave is as good as it is going to get. But he makes a discovery. He has a refuge.

Sometimes you are in a cave, and no human action is able to get you out. There is something you can't fix, can't heal, or can't escape, and all you can do is trust God. Finding ultimate refuge in God means you become so immersed in his presence, so convinced of his goodness, so devoted to his lordship that you find even the cave is a perfectly safe place to be because he is there with you.

A friend of mine, who attended the same graduate school in psychology, wanted to get married. He was quite healthy himself emotionally but seemed to attract dating partners who were lacking. This became discouraging after a while. He was in the dating cave. When he became a university professor, he used to teach abnormal psychology with a twist: He would illustrate each major category of psychopathology by describing one of his old girlfriends. It was one of the most highly attended classes on campus. He refused to make a foolish choice—he just patiently waited on God.

I remember when he finally met the girl who would become his wife—she was a vibrant, devoted Christian and an emotionally healthy person with superb relational skills. She, like him, had a Ph.D. in clinical psychology. My friend finally emerged from the cave. But it was not the last time he would find himself there.

After they were married, the two of them wanted to have children very much. But because she had breast cancer, it looked as though it would not happen. It was cave time again. But then she recovered! Their time in the cave was over. Eventually they had a beautiful baby girl.

I moved to another part of the country. A few years later they had another child. Then one day I received a phone call. After seven years, the breast cancer had returned. This time it was in her bones and inoperable. And on the answering machine, when she left the message, along with the pain, anxiety, and fear, this is what she expressed: "I have never felt God's presence more strongly or have been more sure of God's goodness than I am now."

Sometimes there is no way out of the cave. In those times all you can do is find refuge in God. Then you come to learn that God knows about caves, because Jesus suffered like us, and for us. The Son of David understood that sinking feeling even more than David did. No one has ever descended the way Jesus did.

The Son of David also lost his position, his status as a teacher, his safety and security. He lost not only his best friend, but all his friends, in spite of his teachings and warnings. His life, too, was endangered. But his failure got worse. He went to a cross and died. All his dreams, and all the dreams he inspired, appeared to die with him. What started as a shining success ended in ignoble failure.

And then they put his body in a cave. That was their big mistake. His body was there for three days. But they could not keep him there. They forgot that God does some of his best work in caves.

The cave is where God resurrects dead things.

I don't know what cave you are in right now.

Maybe it is a lost job. Maybe it is a failed marriage. Maybe a child whom you love has disappointed you. Maybe your dreams for children look as if they will never be fulfilled. Maybe it has become apparent that the greatest longing of your life will never see the light of day.

> God does some of his best work in caves. The cave is where God resurrects dead things.

Maybe you are not in a cave at all. Maybe you never have been. But you will.

Sooner or later, everybody logs some time in the cave. So when your time comes, just remember one thing: God does some of his best work in caves.

GETTING OUT OF THE BOAT

1. How did your parents and family model "failure management" for you?
2. What would you say is your most common response to failure?
   - ❏ Shame
   - ❏ Fear
   - ❏ Increased determination
   - ❏ Denial
   - ❏ Blaming someone else
   - ❏ Other

   Why?
3. What has been the most painful failure of your life? How has it affected you?
4. Where might fear of failure be holding you back today?
5. How adept are you at "encouraging yourself in the Lord"? How might you develop your ability to do this more effectively?

failure - situation where a person's expectations have not been met.

Jesus immediately reached out his hand and caught him, saying to him, "You of little faith, why did you doubt?"

Matthew 14:31

Focusing on Jesus

Each of us carries a word in his heart, a "no" or a "yes."

Martin Seligman

For in him every one of God's promises is a "Yes."

2 Corinthians 1:20

The first time I ever skied was in the Swiss Alps. A friend who ran a winter sports camp flew my wife and me from Scotland, where we were living on the meager funds of a graduate fellowship, paid for our ski rentals, and bought us lift tickets. After two trips down the bunny slope, I told my wife, an avid skier, that I was ready for something more adventurous. We got on a chair lift, and it quickly rose hundreds of feet off the ground. My wife, you may remember, does not like heights. She grabbed the metal pole that stood between us and wrapped herself around it like a boa constrictor.

"Honey," she said, paraphrasing Ken Davis. "I love you. You're my husband, and I'd do anything for you. But do you see this post? This is *my* post. If you touch this post, you'll meet Jesus today."

"Don't look down," I suggested.

We got off the chair lift and took something called a T-bar up the final ascent. Unfortunately, when we were almost to the top of the mountain, we fell off the T-bar. For a while we lay in the snow, waiting for the St. Bernard who never came. Dozens of skiers whizzed up the Alp beside us, yelling advice to us in German. The only word I could make out was "Dumköpf."

Another couple fell off (or jumped out of pity) at the same point. Hans could speak a little English, and he guided us in an hour through hip-deep snow to the nearest slope. The slope was marked by a black diamond with skull and crossbones. It went downhill at an angle of about eighty-five degrees.

Hans then gave me the only skiing lesson I have ever had. "Don't look down," he said. "You will be frightened by the slope and overwhelmed by the distance. When new skiers look down, they panic; and when they face straight ahead on a slope this steep—" He made a whistling sound and a motion with his hand that was not encouraging; it was vaguely reminiscent of the "agony of defeat" guy on the old television program *Wide World of Sports*. "I think you can make it." (The word *think* bothered me a little.) "Just remember one thing: Don't look down."

"Don't look down" became the number one rule in my life. I would not look down for anything. Six-year-old skiers would ski between my legs to try to tempt me to watch them go down. I set a record for Most Zigzag Turns that day. People would ski past me, take the chair lift up, go past me again—just to see how many times they could lap me.

I suspect I pulled off the ugliest ski run that particular Alp had ever seen. Even when making snowplow turns, I would arrange whenever possible to execute them in front of small children so they could break my fall if necessary.

I got only one thing right: I never looked down. I became the world's expert at not looking down. It wasn't pretty, but it got me to the bottom of the hill.

＊ When Peter was walking on the water, the text does not tell us whether Jesus said anything to him or not. But if he did, I imagine it being along these lines: *Peter, whatever you do—don't look down. Keep going, one foot in front of the other. Think light thoughts! Just remember, whatever you do—don't look down.* I imagine that Peter's eyes were locked on Jesus—that during this experience an awareness of Jesus simply dominated Peter's mind. Like master, like disciple.

At any rate, for however long it lasted, Peter walked on the water. Then we are told three things happened. The focus of his attention shifted from Jesus to the storm—he saw the wind. This shift in attention gave rise to a new set of thoughts and feelings that focused on panic and inadequacy: "He became frightened." This in turn disrupted his ability to continue walking in Jesus' power—he began to sink and cried out, "Lord, save me!"

I am reminded of those cartoon characters who occasionally run off a cliff without noticing it—like Wile E. Coyote in the Roadrunner cartoons. For a while he continues to pump his legs and actually runs as well on thin air as he had on the ground. Then suddenly he notices he has run off a cliff. He panics, holds up a little sign, *Save me*, and plummets thousands of feet to what would be the death of an ordinary coyote, but only leaves him with a few bruises, which are gone by the next frame. Apparently it is not running off the cliff that did him in—the fall started when he *noticed*. He forgot rule number one: Don't look down.

When Jesus rescued him, he asked Peter why he doubted. I do not think this was simply an exercise in blaming. I think that, like any good teacher, Jesus really did want Peter to learn from this experience so he could grow.

Hope Is the Fuel

Matthew seems to want us to understand something clearly. While Peter's mind was focused on Jesus, he was empowered to walk on the water. But when his focus was on the storm, his fear short-circuited his ability to receive God's sustaining power.

Hope got Peter out of the boat.

Trust held him up.

Fear sank him.

Everything hinged on whether he was focused on the Savior or on the storm.

There is a condition of the mind that is essential for us to live the kind of lives we are longing for. Call it hope, trust, or confidence. It is the single greatest difference between those who try and those who give up. When it is lost, like Peter we are sunk. *Don't look down.*

Hope is the fuel that the human heart runs on. A car crash or a diving accident can paralyze a body, but the death of hope paralyzes the spirit.

Hope is what prompts a young man and woman to stand before a preacher and promise "I do" even though they have no guarantees.

Hope is what fuels the same couple, many years later, after broken promises and broken hearts, to give their promise another try.

Hope is why human beings keep bringing children into a fallen world.

Hope is why there are hospitals and universities.

Hope is why there are therapists and consultants and why the Cubs keep going to spring training.

No composer would agonize over a score without the hope that some glimmer of beauty will emerge from the struggle.

No parents would agonize over a child without the hope that the child might live a better, nobler, happier life than they did.

When he was an old man, the master painter Henri Matisse was crippled by arthritis. Wrapping his fingers around a brush was painful; painting was agony. Someone asked him why he kept painting. He answered, "The pain goes away; the beauty endures." That is hope.

Pablo Casals continued to practice the cello five hours a day even though he was recognized as the world's greatest cellist, even when he had grown ancient enough that the effort exhausted him. Someone asked him what made him do it. "I think I'm getting better." That is hope.

Lewis Smedes writes that when Michelangelo was laboring day after day painting the ceiling of the Sistine Chapel, he grew so discouraged that he resolved to quit.

> As the dusk darkened the always-shadowed Sistine Chapel, Michelangelo, weary, sore, and doubtful, climbed down the ladder from his scaffolding where he'd been lying on his back since dawn painting the chapel ceiling. After eating a lonely dinner, he wrote a sonnet to his aching body. The last line [was] ... *I'm no painter.*
>
> But when the sun shone again, Michelangelo got up from his bed, climbed up his scaffold, and labored another day on his magnificent vision of the Creator.

What pushed him up the ladder? Hope.

The story of every character God uses in the Bible is the story of hope.

Hope is what made Abraham leave his home.

Hope is what made Moses willing to take on Pharaoh.

Hope is what drove the prophets to keep taking on city hall.

We can survive the loss of an extraordinary number of things, but no one can outlive hope. When it is gone, we are done. Therefore the capacity to stay focused on the presence and power of God in our lives becomes supremely important. When we forget this simple truth, we are like a steelworker walking on an I-beam three hundred feet in the air who begins looking down. When we become more focused on the overwhelming nature of the storm than the overwhelming presence of God, we are in trouble. The Bible speaks of this often in terms of "losing heart."

Whenever Jesus calls someone to get out of the boat, he gives the power to walk on the water. Remember St. Jerome's words: "You command, and immediately the waters are solid." He never calls people to sink. It will surely happen sometimes—but it is not his intent; his call is never a set-up for failure.

Moses sent out twelve scouts to explore the Promised Land, to look at their enemies—people who defied God. Ten came back and said, "The people there are like giants. We'd better turn around and go home." Two—Joshua and Caleb—said, "We should go up and take possession of the land, for we can certainly do it."

> Whenever Jesus calls someone to get out of the boat, he gives the power to walk on the water.

All twelve looked at same land, faced the same situation, and reached two diametrically opposed conclusions.

A young shepherd boy brought supplies to his brothers, who were serving in the army. The great champion of their enemies, a giant named Goliath, a character out of the World Wrestling Federation, was taunting them. All the soldiers saw him and were too terrified to challenge him; they lost heart. David saw him and went after him with a slingshot.

Jesus and the disciples were in a boat when a storm came up. The disciples were so frightened, they were convinced they were going to die; crying out in panic, they lost heart. Jesus sat in the same boat, rode out the same storm—and took a nap.

In all these stories, two sets of people faced exactly the same situation. They scouted the same Promised Land, faced the same enemy, endured the same storm. Some responded with peace, some with panic. Some lost heart, and some took heart.

Don't look down.

Learned Helplessness

Let's look at this matter of heart for a moment in contemporary terms. What is the common denominator in the ten fearful spies and the Israelite soldiers who were paralyzed by Goliath?

One of the most influential psychology experiments of the twentieth century involved precisely this issue. Martin Seligman was a graduate student at the University of Pennsylvania in the 1960s when he stumbled onto an interesting phenomenon called "learned helplessness." It happened when some dogs were given slight electric shocks over which they had no control—no matter what the dogs did, they could not stop the shocks. The shocks simply stopped at random.

Later the dogs were placed in a situation where they could *easily* stop the shocks. They were put in a box that had a low barrier in the middle of it; all they had to do was step over the barrier to the other side and the shocks would stop. Ordinarily dogs learn to do this very quickly. When they are shocked, they start jumping around and discover that crossing the barrier brings relief. However, these previously shocked dogs had apparently learned something different—they "learned" that they were powerless to stop the shocks. They came to believe that no matter how hard they tried, nothing they did would make a difference. So they stopped trying. They lay down and refused to move even though a few steps would have made all the difference in the world.

❋ Seligman describes the phenomenon this way: *"Learned helplessness is the giving up reaction, the quitting response that follows from the belief that whatever you do doesn't matter."*

Hope makes an extraordinary difference. Academic performance of freshmen at the University of Pennsylvania were predicted more accurately by tests that measured their level of optimism than by their SAT scores or high school grades. Daniel Goleman writes, "From the perspective of emotional intelligence, having hope means that one will not give in to overwhelming anxiety, a defeatist attitude, or depression in the face of difficult challenges or setbacks. Indeed, people who are hopeful evidence less depression than others as they maneuver through life in pursuit of their goals, are less anxious in general, and have fewer emotional distresses." The conviction that our effort makes a difference and that we are not victims of circumstance is what keeps us persisting in the face of setbacks. It saves us from apathy, hopelessness, and despair.

Hope does not just motivate positive action. It actually has healing power. In one study, 122 men who had suffered their first heart attack were evaluated on their degree of hopefulness and pessimism. Of the 25 most pessimistic men, 21 had died eight years later. Of the 25 most optimistic, only 6 had died! Loss of hope increased the odds of death more than 300 percent; it predicted death more accurately than any medical risk factor including blood pressure, amount of damage to the heart, or cholesterol level. Better to eat Twinkies in hope than to eat broccoli in despair.

Gordon MacDonald quotes historian John Keegan to the effect that the battles of the Somme and Ypres in World War I—battles in which 240,000 British soldiers were killed or wounded—marked the end of an age of "vital optimism," from which Great Britain has never recovered. Vital optimism, MacDonald says, is "a quality of spirit possessed by a community or person where there is a persuasion that the best is yet to be." The adjective is telling because of two ways in which we use *vital:* it is urgent because we have lost something of great importance, but it is also related to our *vitality*—to a quality of liveliness and energy. To the extent that we lack vital optimism, we cease to be fully alive.

Christ-Mastery

When someone comes to believe in God, to believe that he really is interested and active in human affairs, the issue of learned helplessness changes radically. Alburt Bandura is a Stanford psychologist who has led research on what is commonly called "self-efficacy"—the belief that I have mastery over events in my life and can handle whatever comes my way. People with a strong sense of self-efficacy are much more likely to be resilient in the face of failure, to cope instead of fear. Self-efficacy is strong confidence in one's abilities.

But for one who believes in God, the hinge point is not simply what *I'm* capable of. The real question is what might God want to do through me. "I can do all things through Christ who gives me strength." Now, this is not a blank check. In writing these words, the apostle Paul did not intend for us to understand that being a Christian means I can hit more home runs than Mark McGwire and hit higher notes than Pavarotti. It means I have great confidence that I can face whatever life throws at me, that I never need to give up, that my efforts have potency—because of the One at work within me.

Here we see that optimism and hope are not quite the same thing. Optimism requires what Christopher Lasch calls a belief in progress—that things will in fact get better for me. Hope includes all the psychological advantages of optimism, but it is rooted in something deeper. When I hope, I believe that God is at work to redeem all things *regardless of how things happen to be turning out for me today*. Hope does not prevent me from expecting the worst—"the worst is what the hopeful are prepared for." The Christ-follower is to be marked by what we might call *vital hope*.

So let's think a while about what it means to cultivate a *mind* that is dominated by this one thought: "I can do all things through Christ who gives me strength." How do we go about developing minds that focus on Christ in the middle of storms?

Immediately we come to an amazing discovery. People (including you and me—at least me) are often astoundingly cavalier about the way they treat their minds.

What is your mind focused on?

Imagine getting the greatest performance car in the world and deciding you are going to take a serious run at the Indy 500 and dedicate yourself to winning it. What are the odds you would fill the tank with unleaded, low-octane gasoline from a thrifty-discount service station?

Imagine you were serious about competing in the marathon in the Olympics. This becomes the all-consuming goal of your life. How likely would you be to go on an all-chocolate diet between now and the games?

When a couple has a child, they are very careful about what goes into that child's mouth. We tend to be very serious about what we put into the things that matter to us. People are very careful about what they feed their cars, their bodies, their children, even their pets.

What you put into your body alone has become a multibillion dollar industry. People spend billions of dollars trying to convince us of what we need. They tell us that the secret to health is a high-carbs, low-fat diet; or high protein, fat is okay, with no carbs at all; or a 30–30–40 percentage split; or avoiding sugar at all costs. They tell us the secret is Atkins bars, Pritikin bars, Met-Rex bars, Power bars, Slim-Fast shakes, Nutri-Fast shakes, wheat-germ shakes, or Chicago-style deep-dish pizza. (No one's come out with that diet yet, but when they do, I'm going to publicly endorse it.)

We are very aware that the fuel that goes into things ultimately determines their performance and well-being. That is why it is so ironic that in the most important area of life we often disregard one basic human resource with a nonchalance that is nothing less than astounding—the mind. What we feed everything else we possess is nothing compared with the importance of what we feed our minds. The apostle Paul wrote, "Whatever is true, whatever is honorable, or whatever is just, whatever is pure, whatever is pleasing, ... think about these things"—or in other words, "feed your minds."

Our ability to live in hope—to remain focused on Christ during the storm—is largely dependent on what we feed our minds. This is how we are able to focus on the Savior rather than the storm.

I want to introduce you to two laws that govern your life. The first is what might be called the *law of cognition:* You are what you think. Psychologist Archibald Hart writes, "Research has shown that one's thought life influences every aspect of one's being." Whether we are filled with confidence or fear depends on the kind of thoughts that habitually occupy our minds.

Over the last thirty years or so, the most dominant movement in American psychology is what is known as cognitive psychology—built around the truth that the way you think is the single most determinative thing about you:

The way you think creates your attitudes; the way you think shapes your emotions; the way you think governs your behavior; the way you think deeply influences your immune system and vulnerability to illness. Everything about you flows out of the way you think.

I believe this is one of those cases where we are simply coming to confirm what the writers of Scripture knew quite clearly all along. Paul said, "Do not be conformed to this world, but be transformed by the renewing of your minds."

Jesus once said that a good tree cannot produce bad fruit, and a bad tree cannot produce good fruit. He was making this observation in terms of the connection between our inward condition and outward behavior. Over the long haul, good thinking—accurate perceptions, healthy emotions, wholesome desires, honorable intentions—cannot produce bad results; bad thinking cannot produce good results.

The second law might be called the *law of exposure:* Your mind will think most about what it is most exposed to. What repeatedly enters your mind occupies your mind, eventually shapes your mind, and will ultimately express itself in what you do and who you become. The law of exposure is as inviolable as the law of gravity. No one is surprised by the law of gravity. No one says, "Hey, I dropped this priceless antique crystal vase on cement and it broke. What are the odds of that?" But amazingly enough, people react to the law of exposure in total shock. People are surprised that what their minds are constantly exposed to, attend to, and dwell on eventually comes out in how they feel and what they do.

Children are exposed to thousands of acts of violence and murder on television and in even more graphic forms in movies. They see it on video games and observe symbols and images associated with gang violence glorified in pop culture—then we act surprised when a fight breaks out in the bleachers at a football game, or when shootings at Columbine High School devastate an entire nation. The truth is, we simply lack the national will and self-restraint to create a society that will produce minds that are not saturated with violence from the cradle on.

We are flooded with sexual images on television screens, computer terminals, magazine covers, and multiplex movie marquees. Sexually explicit images and e-mails are sent not just to teenagers, but to children who have virtually no chance to protect themselves from what they do not even know they are getting into—and then we profess to be shocked when promiscuity and sexual addiction levels go up and marital fidelity and stability go down.

It is amazing to me how often people think or live as if they could get away with violating the law of exposure. People will say, "I can read this material, watch these images, or listen to these twisted words—but it doesn't really affect me. I'm not really paying attention. It goes in one ear and out the other." Social scientists are coming to realize what writers of Scripture knew all along: Oh no, it doesn't!

If enough teenage girls look at enough magazine covers featuring enough models who are paid outrageous sums of money to make themselves unnaturally thin and then interviewed and quoted as the experts on what makes life worth living, we will raise a generation of young women whose minds are constantly filled with such thoughts: You're not thin enough, not pretty enough, not desirable enough to men. Their feelings of self-esteem will plummet. Hope will die. And the behavioral consequences will skyrocket—and it shouldn't surprise anyone.

The events you attend, the material you read (or don't), the music you hear, the images you watch, the conversations you hold, the daydreams you entertain—all are shaping your mind and, ultimately, your character and destiny. This is supremely true when it comes to hope.

Isaiah says, "Thou wilt keep him in perfect peace, whose mind is stayed on thee." It all depends on where your mind stays. The good news is that you can put these laws to work *for* you. If you really want to become a certain kind of person—a hopeful person focused on Christ—you must begin to think thoughts

> If you really want to become a certain kind of person—a hopeful person focused on Christ—you must begin to think thoughts that will produce those characteristics.

that will produce those characteristics. So we understand why Paul said, "Think about these things." When you focus on Christ, these are the kinds of thoughts he will inspire you to think. Therefore you must put your mind in a place that will lead you to think hope-producing thoughts. You need to expose your mind to those resources, books, tapes, people, and conversations that will incline you toward confidence in God. How does this happen?

Undiscovered Continents of Spiritual Living

Frank Laubach devoted his whole life to learning to focus on Jesus. He was a sociologist, educator, and missionary to the Philippines in the early twentieth century whose career fell apart when he was in his forties. He lost the vocational opportunity he most desired. His plans for the Maranao people of the Philippines were utterly rejected. He and his wife lost three children to malaria, so she took their remaining child and moved a thousand miles away, leaving him desperately lonely.

In deep despair Laubach took his dog Tip and went to the top of Signal Hill, which overlooks Lake Lanao. He wrote,

> Tip had his nose up under my arm and was trying to lick the tears off my cheeks. My lips began to move and it seemed to me that God was speaking.
>
> *"My child . . . you have failed because you do not really love these Maranaos. You feel superior to them because you are white. If you forget you are an American and think only how I love them, they will respond."*
>
> I answered back to the sunset, "God, I don't know whether you spoke to me through my lips, but if you did, it was the truth. My plans have all gone to pieces. Drive me out of myself and come and take possession of me and think thy thoughts in my mind."

This was the beginning of one of the remarkable spiritual experiments of the twentieth century. Laubach devoted the rest of his life to seeking to live each moment in conscious awareness of God's presence and carrying on a rich friendship with him.

Here are some thoughts based on his recommendations for staying focused on Christ:

—In a social setting, whisper "God" or "Jesus" quietly as you glance at each person near you. Practice "double vision" as Christ does—see the person as he is and the person as Christ wants him to be.

—At mealtime, have an extra chair at the table to remind you of the presence of Christ. As you see it, or touch it, remember his words: "Lo, I am with you always...."

—While reading a book or magazine—read it to him! Laubach asks, "Have you ever opened a letter [or more likely clicked on e-mail these days] and read it with Jesus, realizing that he smiles with us at the fun, rejoices with us in the successes, and weeps with us in the tragedies? If not, you have missed one of life's sweetest experiences."

—When problem-solving at work, instead of talking to yourself about the problem, develop a new habit of talking to Christ. (This is, after all, what Peter did with his problem of sinking.) As Laubach says, "Many of us who have tried this have found that we think so much better that we never want to try to think without Him again!"

—Keep a picture of Christ or a cross or a word from Scripture someplace where you will see it just as you're going to sleep. Allow God to have the last word of the day. Then let your eyes and mind begin there in the morning. Laubach writes, "As we open our eyes and see a picture of Christ on the wall we may ask: 'Now, Master, shall we get up?' [If you're not a 'morning person,' you may need a definite word from the Lord on this question.] Some of us whisper to him our every thought about washing and dressing in the morning, about brushing our shoes

> "Christ is interested in every trifle, because He loves us more intimately than a mother loves her babe."
>
> —Frank Laubach

and choosing our clothes. Christ is interested in every tri-fle, because He loves us more intimately than a mother loves her babe...."

The power of such practices, Laubach discovered, is not simply that they changed the patterns of his mind, though that in itself has considerable power. The real significance of this way of life is that it opened him wide to spiritual reality and power that was in fact all around him all the time, like a radio antenna suddenly tuned in to the right frequency. It convinced him that there are, as he put it in one wonderful phrase, "undiscovered continents of spiritual living" available to any who would diligently open themselves up to them.

Laubach's extraordinary practice of focusing on Christ, begun in his mid-forties, led to a remarkable life. He became perhaps the most influential literacy advocate of his time, traveling to 103 countries to lead a worldwide literacy program. He founded the World Literacy Crusade, which is still in operation. He developed the "Each One Teach One" program that continues to this day. Without formal appointment, he became an influential foreign policy adviser to U.S. presidents during the post-World War II years. He wrote books about focusing on Christ that have sold hundreds of thousands of copies. He walked on the water.

But the art he really mastered was focusing on Christ.

Meditation on Scripture

Scripture talks about meditating on God's Word. The psalmist says that godly persons meditate on the Word "day and night." How much is that?

You may feel that meditation is something only monks and mystics can do. So let me ask, do you know how to worry? If you can worry, you can meditate. To meditate merely means to think about something over and over. Let it simmer in your mind. Reflect on it from different angles until it becomes part of you.

Memorizing Scripture is an important part of keeping a mind focused on Christ. This is a scary thought for many people. Maybe you are quite good at this; maybe you have happy memories of studying for school tests—you looked at something once and it became lodged in your mind like the Rock of Gibraltar. But maybe not. Maybe you find memorizing hard work. You have a hard time finding your car at mall parking lots; it takes you two or three attempts to get your child's name right (and you only have one child).

> **Memorizing Scripture is an important part of keeping a mind focused on Christ.**

The point of memorizing Scripture is not to see how many verses you can memorize. The point is what happens to your mind in the process of rehearsing Scripture. When you are rehearsing statements from Scripture, you are having different thoughts than you would be if you were watching some television show.

A friend recently sent me a card that read, "May the God of hope fill you with all joy and peace as you trust in him, so that you may overflow with hope by the power of the Holy Spirit."

When I think about that single statement, I am reminded that

—God is the source of all hope;
—He is even now seeking to fill my body with not just joy and peace, but *all* joy and peace;
—His desire is that I should not just contain hope, but *overflow* with hope;
—This process is dependent not on my power, but the power of the Holy Spirit at work in me.

My mind is having different thoughts than it would be if I were reading the *National Enquirer*. With my mind fixed on God, I am ready to get out of the boat.

Keep Your Fork

One of the most important tools for focusing our minds involves rituals. I grew up in a tradition that was suspicious about the use of "ritual" in spiritual life, but in fact, rituals are generally indispensable for healthy human living.

A recent book for "corporate athletes" found that those who performed at the highest level used, among other things, a series of rituals

— do this in remembrance of me

that helped focus their minds and energies and enabled them to be fully
present to their work.

Psychologists tell us that people develop rituals for whatever
things are important to them. When a family or marriage is ritual-
poor, it often means the relationship is in trouble.

cannot be mindless rituals.

So I have appropriated certain rituals and symbols that help keep
my mind focused on Christ:

—I have a nail in my office, about the size of the nails that
might have been used on the cross. Sometimes in prayer I
will hold it to remind me of what Jesus suffered for me.

—I have a statue of a little child, whose arms are wrapped
around a loving father. I look at that when I pray, and I
think of God loving me like that.

—I have a stone with a single word on it. It was given to me
by a very good friend, who said that this is a quality that
he sees in my life. I don't see this quality much in me, but I
want very much to see it. This is a word from God for me,
and sometimes I pray about this word.

—I have a great prayer, framed for me and placed on the wall.
It is attributed to St. Patrick many centuries ago. It is called
"Lorica"—named for a Roman coat of armor that is meant
for the protection of the one wearing it:

I arise today through God's strength to pilot me:
God's might to uphold me,
God's wisdom to guide me,
God's eye to look before me
God's ear to hear me,
God's word to speak for me,
God's hand to guard me.
Christ with me, Christ before me, Christ behind me,
Christ in me, Christ beneath me, Christ above me,
Christ on my right, Christ on my left,
Christ when I lie down, Christ when I sit down, Christ
when I arise.
Christ in the heart of every one who thinks of me,

Christ in the mouth of every one who speaks of me,
Christ in every eye that sees me,
Christ in every ear that hears me.
I arise today
Through a mighty strength, the invocation of the Trinity.

I think of this as the armor of King Saul that David tried to put on when he went to fight Goliath, even though it did not fit him (Saul being a fifty long and David being a thirty-six short). And I ask God to shield me in it as well.

A friend of mine travels quite a lot in his business. When he gets to his motel room, the first thing he does is place a picture of his wife and children on the television set. One reason he does this is that sometimes he will be tempted to turn on adult movies. He knows they would shape his mind in ways he does not desire. When he looks at his family, he has other thoughts. Some of them are guilty thoughts about his vulnerability to temptation and past failures. But mostly they are thoughts about how much he loves his family and about the kind of father and husband he wants to be. The pictures remind him of his hope, and hope gives him strength.

What does a mind that is focused on hope look like? I read recently about a woman who had been diagnosed with cancer and was given three months to live. Her doctor told her to make preparations to die, so she contacted her pastor and told him how she wanted things arranged for her funeral service—which songs she wanted to have sung, what Scriptures should be read, what words should be spoken—and that she wanted to be buried with her favorite Bible.

But before he left, she called out to him, "*One more thing.*"
"What?"
"*This is important. I want to be buried with a fork in my right hand.*" The pastor did not know what to say. No one had ever made such a request before. So she explained. "In all my years going to church functions, whenever food was involved, my favorite part was when whoever was cleaning dishes of the main course would lean over and say, *You can keep your fork.*

"It was my favorite part because I knew that it meant something great was coming. It wasn't Jell-O. It was something with substance—cake or pie—biblical food.

"So I just want people to see me there in my casket with a fork in my hand, and I want them to wonder, *What's with the fork?* Then I want you to tell them, *Something better is coming. Keep your fork.*"

The pastor hugged the woman good-bye. And soon after, she died.

At the funeral service people saw the dress she had chosen, saw the Bible she loved, and heard the songs she loved, but they all asked the same question: "What's with the fork?"

The pastor explained that this woman, their friend, wanted them to know that for her—or for anyone who dies in Christ—this is not a day of defeat. It is a day of celebration. The real party is just starting.

Something better is coming.

So this week why not make the humble fork your own personal icon? Each time you sit down to a meal, take a look at the utensil on the left side of your plate, and remember the woman who took one to her casket. When you pause to give thanks for the food, give thanks for your hope as well. Each time you wrap your fingers around the handle of a fork, remember: "Something better is coming."

Remember that the God of water-walking and empty tombs has a message for you. Jesus says to all who labor and are heavy laden:

To all who get discouraged or fall into temptation,

To anyone whose mind ever strays to dreamless trifles,

To people like you and me who are tempted to despair or lose hope,   He still says,

Don't look down.

Keep your fork.

GETTING OUT OF THE BOAT

1. Pay attention to where your mind drifts today. How would you describe the kind of thoughts you are most often pulled toward?

   Fear

   Hope

Anger
Sorrow
Apathy
Joy
Discouragement
Other

2. What sources (media, books, friends, activities) most *damage* your level of hope?
3. What sources (media, books, friends, activities) most *feed* your level of hope?
4. In light of this, how might you want to rearrange your life to create the highest level of hope possible?
5. Set aside one day and make it your goal to spend as much of it with Jesus as possible. Invite him to be part of each activity. Invent rituals and use objects (like the fork) to help you maintain focus.
6. How did it go?

CHAPTER 9

When they got into the boat, the wind ceased.

Matthew 14:32

Learning to Wait

●

Waiting is the hardest work of hope.

Lewis Smedes

Waiting patiently is not a strong suit in American society.

A woman's car stalls in traffic. She looks in vain under the hood to identify the cause, while the driver behind her leans relentlessly on his horn. Finally she has had enough. She walks back to his car and offers sweetly, "I don't know what the matter is with my car. But if you want to go look under the hood, I'll be glad to stay here and honk for you."

We are not a patient people. We tend to be in a horn-honking, microwaving, Fed-Ex mailing, fast-food eating, express-lane shopping hurry. People don't like to wait in traffic, on the phone, in the store, or at the post office.

Robert Levine, in a wonderful book called *A Geography of Time*, suggests the creation of a new unit of time called the *honko-second*—"the time between when the light changes and the person behind you honks his horn." He claims it is the smallest measure of time known to science.

So how well do you wait?

At a tollbooth, the driver of the car in front of you is having an extended conversation with the tollbooth operator. You—

A. Are happy they are experiencing the tollbooth in community. You think about joining them and forming a small group.
B. Dream of things you would like to say to the tollbooth operator.
C. Attempt to drive your vehicle between the other guy's car and the tollbooth.

You have been sitting in the waiting room of your doctor's office for an hour. You—

A. Are grateful for the chance to catch up on the 1993 *Reader's Digest.*
B. Tell the other patients you have a highly contagious and fatal disease, hoping this will empty the waiting room.
C. Force yourself to hyperventilate to get immediate attention.

Most of us do not like waiting very much, so we like the fact that Matthew shows Jesus to be the Lord of urgent action. Three times in just a few sentences Matthew uses the word *immediately*—always of Jesus: Jesus made the disciples get into a boat and go on ahead of him "immediately." When the disciples thought they were seeing a ghost and cried out in fear, Jesus answered them "immediately." When Peter began to sink and cried out for help, Jesus "immediately" reached out his hand and caught him.

Jesus' actions are swift, discerning, and decisive. He doesn't waste a honko-second. And yet, this is also a story about waiting. Matthew tells us that Jesus comes to the disciples "during the fourth watch of the night." The Romans divided the night into four shifts: 6:00–9:00; 9:00-midnight; midnight–3:00; and 3:00–6:00. So Jesus came to the disciples sometime after 3 o'clock. But they had been in the boat since before sundown the previous day. Why the long delay? If I were one of the disciples, I think I would prefer Jesus to show up at the same time or even slightly ahead of the storm. I'd like him there in a honko-second.

But Matthew has good reasons for noting the time. A. E. J. Rawlinson notes that early Christians suffering their own storm of persecution may have taken great comfort in this delay:

> Faint hearts may even have begun to wonder whether the Lord Himself had not abandoned them to their fate, or to

doubt the reality of Christ. They are to learn from this story that they are not forsaken, that the Lord watches over them unseen ... [that] the Living One, Master of wind and waves, will surely come quickly for their salvation, even though it be in the "fourth watch of the night."

Matthew wanted his readers to learn to wait.

Another moment of waiting involves Peter's decision to leave the boat. He cannot do this on the strength of his own impulse; he must ask Jesus' permission first, then wait for an answer—for the light to turn green. One of the biggest differences between a Type T and Type W is that W's learn to wait.

I wonder if another type of waiting was involved for Peter. What do you suppose his very first steps on the water looked like? I expect that Jesus was an accomplished water-walker. But for Peter, I wonder if there wasn't a learning curve involved. Maybe, like the Bill Murray character in the movie *What About Bob?*, he had to start with baby steps. Learning to walk always requires patience.

It was not until the whole episode was over that the disciples got what they wanted—"the wind died down." Why couldn't Jesus have made the wind die down "immediately"—as soon as he saw the disciples' fear? It would have made Peter's walk easier. But apparently Jesus felt they would gain something by waiting.

So, in this next-to-last chapter, before you rush out to walk on the water, I want you to consider the activity that Peter and the other disciples had to engage in right up to the very end: waiting.

Let's say you decide to get out of the boat. You trust God. You take a step of faith—you courageously choose to leave a comfortable job to devote yourself to God's calling; you will use a gift you believe God has given you even though you are scared to death; you will take relational risks even though you hate rejection; you will go back to school even though people tell you it makes no sense financially; you decide to trust God and get out of the boat. What happens next?

Well, maybe you will experience a tremendous, nonstop rush of excitement. Maybe there will be an immediate confirmation of your decision—circumstances will click, every risk will pay off, your efforts will be crowned with success, your spiritual life will thrive, your faith will double, and your friends will marvel, all in the space of a honko-second.

Maybe. But not always. For good reasons, God does not always move at our frantic pace. We are too often double espresso followers of a decaf Sovereign. Richard Mouw writes that the book that is most needed in our day would be called *Your God Is Too Fast*.

Some forms of waiting—on expressways and in doctor's offices—are fairly trivial in the overall scheme of things. But there are more serious and difficult kinds of waiting:

—The waiting of a single person who hopes God might have marriage in store but is beginning to despair

—The waiting of a childless couple who desperately want to start a family

—The waiting of Nelson Mandela as he sits in a prison cell for twenty-seven years and wonders if he will ever be free or if his country will ever know justice

—The waiting of someone who longs to have work that is meaningful and significant and yet cannot seem to find it

—The waiting of a deeply depressed person for a morning when she will wake up wanting to live

—The waiting of a child who feels awkward and clumsy and longs for the day when he gets picked first on the playground

—The waiting of persons of color for the day when everyone's children will be judged "not by the color of their skin but by the content of their character"

—The waiting of an elderly senior citizen in a nursing home—alone, seriously ill, just waiting to die

Every one of us, at some junctures of our lives, will have to learn to wait.

Lewis Smedes writes,

> Waiting is our destiny as creatures who cannot by themselves bring about what they hope for.
>
> We wait in the darkness for a flame we cannot light,

We wait in fear for a happy ending we cannot write.
We wait for a not yet that feels like a not ever.
Waiting is the hardest work of hope.

Waiting may be the hardest single thing we are called to do. So it is frustrating when we turn to the Bible and find that God himself, who is all-powerful and all-wise, keeps saying to his people, *Wait*. "Be still before the LORD, and wait patiently for him.... Wait for the LORD, and keep to his way, and he will exalt you to inherit the land."

God comes to Abraham when he is seventy-five and tells him he is going to be a father, the ancestor of a great nation. How long was it before that promise was fulfilled? Twenty-four years. Abraham had to wait.

God told the Israelites that they would leave their slavery in Egypt and become a nation. But the people had to wait four hundred years.

God told Moses he would lead the people to the Promised Land. But they had to wait forty years in the wilderness.

In the Bible, waiting is so closely associated with faith that sometimes the two words are used interchangeably. The great promise of the Old Testament was that a Messiah would come. But Israel had to wait—generation after generation, century after century. And when *the* Messiah came, he was recognized only by those who had their eyes fixed on his coming—like Simeon. He was an old man who "was righteous and devout. He was *waiting* for the consolation of Israel, and the Holy Spirit was upon him."

But even the arrival of Jesus did not mean that the waiting was over. Jesus lived, taught, was crucified, was resurrected, and was about to ascend when his friends asked him, "Lord, will you restore the kingdom now?" That is, "Can we stop waiting?"

And Jesus had one more command: "Do not leave Jerusalem, but *wait* for the gift my Father promised."

And the Holy Spirit came—but that still did not mean that the time of waiting was over.

Paul wrote, "We ourselves, who have the first fruits of the Spirit, groan inwardly while we wait for adoption, the redemption of our bodies. For in hope we were saved. Now hope that is seen is not hope.

For who hopes for what is seen? But if we hope for what we do not see, we wait for it with patience."

Forty-three times in the Old Testament alone, the people are commanded, "Wait. Wait on the LORD."

The last words in the Bible are about waiting: "The one who testifies to these things says, 'Surely I am coming soon.'" *It may not seem like it, but in light of eternity, it is soon. Hang on.*

"Amen. Come, Lord Jesus!" *All right, we'll hang on. But come! We're waiting for you.*

Why? Why does God make us wait? If he can do anything, why doesn't he bring us relief and help and answers *now?*

At least in part, to paraphrase Ben Patterson, what God does in us while we wait is as important as what it is we are waiting for.

A Water-Walker's Most Important Skill

The ability to wait well is a test of maturity. Psychologists speak of this as the ability to endure delayed gratification. M. Scott Peck writes, "Delaying gratification is a process of scheduling the pain and pleasure of life in such a way as to enhance the pleasure by meeting and experiencing the pain first and getting it over with. It is the only decent way to live."

Daniel Goleman has written a highly influential book in which he argues that effectiveness in life is based not nearly so much on cognitive intelligence as on what might be called "emotional intelligence." This is what can cause people with high IQs to end up in failed marriages or frustrating vocations. At the heart of emotional intelligence is the ability to delay gratification and not live at the mercy of impulse.

The most celebrated example of this phenomenon is what has come to be called the "marshmallow test." A four-year-old is in a room with some marshmallows and told that the experimenter has to run an errand. If the four-year-old can wait till the experimenter returns, he can have two marshmallows. If he wants to eat right now, he can—but he only gets one. This will try the soul of any four-year-old—"a microcosm of the eternal battle between impulse and restraint, id and ego, desire and control, gratification and delay."

Kids would develop all kinds of strategies to enable them to wait— sing songs, tell themselves stories, play with their fingers. One kid actually bent down and began to lick the table, as if the flavor had perhaps transmogrified into the wood. What is most amazing is the impact this one character trait displayed at the age of four had on the lives of those who were part of this experiment. A Stanford University research team tracked these children for many years. Those who were able to wait as four-year-olds grew up to be more socially competent, better able to cope with stress, and less likely to give up under pressure than those who could not wait. The marshmallow-grabbers grew up to be more stubborn and indecisive, more easily upset by frustration, and more resentful about not getting enough. Most amazingly, the group of marshmallow-waiters had SAT scores that averaged *210 points higher* than the group of marshmallow-grabbers!

Moreover, all those years later, the marshmallow-grabbers still were unable to put off gratification. And studies have shown that poor impulse control is much more likely to be associated with delinquency, substance abuse, and divorce. No wonder Goleman, in summarizing all this, calls the ability to wait well "the master aptitude."

The inability to control impulses, the refusal to live in patient waiting and trust, lies close to the heart of human fallenness. Life has been that way since Adam and Eve took a bite from the forbidden marshmallow.

Paul says that while we are waiting for God to set everything right, we suffer. But suffering produces endurance; endurance, character; and character, hope. God is producing these qualities in us as we wait. Waiting is not just something we have to do while we get what we want. It is part of the process of becoming what God wants us to be.

What does it mean to wait on the Lord? Let's start with a word about what biblical waiting is *not*. It is not a passive waiting around for something to happen that will allow you to escape your trouble. People sometimes say, "I'm just waiting on the Lord," as an excuse not to face up to reality, own up to their responsibility, or take appropriate action.

I have heard people with horrible financial habits—impulsive spending, refusal to save—in the midst of a big money mess say, "We're waiting for the Lord to provide...." This fits into the general theological category of *Don't be stupid!* Waiting on the Lord in this case does not mean sitting around hoping you get a letter from Visa that reads, "Bank error in your favor, collect $200." It probably means dragging your little financial self to a source where you can learn biblical principles for a life of good stewardship. It may mean cultivating new financial habits like budgeting, tithing, and putting off buying things until you actually have enough money to pay for them. Biblical waiting is not passive; it is not a way to evade unpleasant reality.

Waiting on the Lord is a confident, disciplined, expectant, active, and sometimes painful clinging to God.

Waiting on the Lord is the continual, daily decision to say, "I will trust you, and I will obey you. Even though the circumstances of my life are not turning out the way I want them to, and may never turn out the way I would choose, I am betting everything on you. I have no plan B."

So what does it take to wait well?

Patient Trust

Waiting on the Lord requires patient trust. Will I trust that God has good reasons for saying "wait"? Will I remember that things look different to God because he views things from an eternal perspective?

Peter wrote, "But do not ignore this one fact, beloved, that with the Lord one day is like a thousand years, and a thousand years are like one day. The Lord is not slow about his promise, as some think of slowness, but is patient with you, not wanting any to perish, but all to come to repentance." The story goes that an economist once read these words and got very excited.

"Lord—is it true that a thousand years for us is just like a minute to you?"

"Yes."

"Then a million dollars to us must just be a penny to you."

"Yes."

"Lord, would you give me one of those pennies?"

"All right. Wait here a minute."

Too often we want God's resources, but we do not want his timing. We want the penny, but not the minute. We forget that his work in us while we wait is as important as what it is we think we are waiting for. Waiting means that we give God the benefit of the doubt that he knows what he is doing.

It must be patient trust—trust that is willing to wait again and again day after day.

Maybe you are single. As Americans we live in a society where so often the assumption is that marriage is normal and being single is not. You feel the pain of that stigma.

Maybe you feel a legitimate longing for intimacy.

Maybe you feel a kind of loneliness that only God can heal, that another human being cannot rescue you from.

Waiting is so hard.

Maybe there is a potential relationship right at your fingertips, but you know it would not be honoring to God. Maybe you know in your heart it is not really the right person because that person does not share your ultimate commitment to God. Maybe that person is putting pressure on you to be involved sexually even though you are not married.

You are tempted to think, "I have been waiting long enough. I'm tired of waiting. I'm going to reach out for whatever satisfaction I can in this life and worry about the consequences later."

Will you wait on the Lord? Will you courageously say, "Okay, God. I will not get hooked up with a relationship that I know would dishonor you and bring damage to the souls of those involved. I will seek to build the best life that I can right where I am, not know-ing what tomorrow holds. Even though I sometimes feel no one else understands how painful it is, I will trust you. I will wait."

Maybe you have a dream about certain accomplishments—it involves your work or an area of ministry. What you hoped for is not happening—you don't know why, but you know it hurts. You are tempted to try to force it—to push, manipulate, or scheme to get what you want.

Or, perhaps you are tempted to give up ever trying to realize the potential God has given you and just drift. Will you have the patience not to force it, not to quit, but to wait patiently, to continue to learn about your giftedness, humbly receive feedback and coaching from others, grow one step at a time, and trust God's plan rather than what you think is your need.

Maybe you are in a difficult relationship. You want to bail emotionally, if not physically. But God is saying, "Wait! Focus on the love you can offer to the other person, not the love you think you have to get back. Trust me. Hang in there. Keep trying."

Having the character to refrain from going for the forbidden marshmallow is one of the toughest tests in the world. But it is worth it.

What does it look like to wait with patient trust?

Henri Nouwen gave us a picture of patient trust not long before he died in 1996. Writing about some trapeze artists who became good friends of his, he explained that there is a very special relationship between the flyer and the catcher. (This does not surprise me. If I were the flyer, I would want to become a very good friend of the catcher. I would work very hard to make sure there were no lingering resentments on his part. I would want the catcher to like me a lot.)

As the flyer is swinging high above the crowd, the moment comes when he lets go of the trapeze, when he arcs out into the air. For that moment, which must feel like an eternity, the flyer is suspended in nothingness. It is too late to reach back for the trapeze. There is no going back now. However, it is too soon to be grasped by the one who will catch him. He cannot accelerate the catch. In that moment, his job is to be as still and motionless as he can.

"The flyer must never try to catch the catcher," the trapeze artist told Nouwen. "He must wait in absolute trust. The catcher will catch him. But he must wait. His job is not to flail about in anxiety. In fact, if he does, it could kill him. His job is to be still. To wait. And to wait is the hardest work of all."

You may be in that very vulnerable moment right now—you have let go of what God has called you to let go of, but you can't feel God's other hand catching you yet. Will you wait in absolute trust? Will you be patient? Waiting requires patient trust.

Confident Humility

Waiting on the Lord also requires confident humility. The prophet said, "The effect of righteousness will be peace, and the result of righteousness, quietness and trust forever."

The result of righteousness, he discerned, will be two character qualities. The first is confidence. And this is not so much confidence in myself as confidence in the One who sustains me. It is the assurance that God is able. It entails a fearless orientation toward the future. The second quality is quietness, the opposite of arrogance and boasting, a humble recognition of my limits.

Waiting is, by its nature, something only the humble can do with grace. When we wait for something, we recognize that we are not in control.

In American society there is a direct correlation between status and waiting. The higher your status, the less you have to wait. Lower-status people always wait on higher-status people.

Try going into doctor's office and saying to the receptionist, "I'm an important person. My time is too valuable to be kept waiting. The doctor must see me at once!" I read recently about a busy CEO who was so frustrated at having to sit in a waiting room that he actually sent the doctor a bill for *his* time.

> Waiting is, by its nature, something only the humble can do with grace.

Waiting is a good thing for people like me. It reminds me that I am not in charge. I'm the patient. I'm in the waiting room. Waiting humbles me in ways I need to be humbled. But in the real issues of life, we are not just waiting around—we are waiting on God. Therefore we can trust his wisdom and timing. We can wait with confidence. Because waiting reminds us that we are waiting *for* someone, the single most important activity in waiting is prayer.

Prayer allows us to wait without worry. One recent night I could not sleep. I was troubled by all kinds of thoughts—"what if " kinds of thoughts. What if this doesn't change? What if something that I desperately want, I don't get? These were frantic voices. There was a semblance of truth to them—bad things can happen—but they did not lead to life.

Not long after that, I was reading the account of Jesus and his friends being in a boat, with a storm lashing them about. The disciples were quite frantic because—remember?—Jesus was sleeping.

And it struck me: There was one experience Jesus never had. He had experienced virtually every human emotion—sorrow, joy, pain. He had been tired, angry, and hopeful. But there was one thing he never experienced: He was never frantic. He never panicked. And in that moment I realized that God is never desperate.

People sometimes talk about recognizing the voice of God when he speaks to them. There is much about this I do not understand. But I do know that the way you learn any person's voice is by experience—a certain tone and quality.

※ God's voice is never frantic. When you hear desperate thoughts, you can know it is not God speaking. You can wait in confident humility.

Waiting on the Lord Requires Inextinguishable Hope

Paul writes, "For in hope we were saved. Now hope that is seen is not hope. For who hopes for what is seen? But if we hope for what we do not see, we *wait* for it with patience."

Hope itself is really a form of waiting. Ernst Hoffmann writes, "New Testament hope is a patient, disciplined, confident waiting for and expectation of the Lord as our Savior.... it demonstrates its living character by the steadfastness with which it waits."

—It is a bridegroom waiting for his bride on their wedding night.

—It is the waiting of a strong man for the race he most loves to run.

—It is waiting for the clock to say 6:00 when it is Christmas morning, and you are seven years old, and your parents told you not to wake them up before 6:00, and you know there's something really good downstairs.

If you are waiting on God these days—if you are obeying him, but you don't see the results you hoped for yet—you need to know that in the Bible there is a wonderful promise attached to this waiting.

Even youths will faint and be weary,
and the young will fall exhausted;
but those who wait for the LORD shall renew their strength,

>they shall mount up with wings like eagles,
>they shall run and not be weary,
>they shall walk and not faint.

I can never forget David Hubbard's comment on these lines. An Old Testament scholar, he was the smartest man I have ever known. Pick any topic—Semitic languages, the history of the Ming Dynasty, engineering innovations, classical music, organizational management theory, baseball statistics—and he could discuss it with experts in the field. Because of his leadership gifts, David spent thirty years as president of the largest interdenominational seminary in the world, but in his heart he was waiting for the day when he could retire from that and devote himself to the study of his first love, the Old Testament. That was the marshmallow he wanted most.

Ironically, very shortly after his retirement he suffered a massive heart attack and died, and so the very opportunity he had waited three decades for appeared to be gone. All of us who knew and loved him were immensely saddened. But it was hard for David to feel sorry for himself. He had always insisted that the point of studying the Book was to get to know the One who stood behind and above it. So the opportunity he had really been waiting for all these years was now finally, fully his.

The last letter I ever got from him, just a few weeks before he died, had a wonderful comment on these lines from Isaiah about waiting. David said that we must live these words—soaring, running, and walking—"one line at a time."

Sometimes you will mount up and soar on wings of eagles. This is a beautiful picture. Ornithologists say birds have three methods of flight. The first is flapping—keeping their wings in constant motion to counteract gravity. Hummingbirds can flap up to seventy times per second. Flapping keeps you up in the air, but it is a lot of work. Flapping is an awkward, clumsy business. I spend a lot of time flapping around. It gets me from here to there, but there is not a lot of grace involved.

A second flight method is gliding. Here the bird builds up enough speed, then coasts downward a while. It is much more graceful than flapping, but unfortunately it does not get the bird very far. Reality in the form of gravity sets in quickly. Gliding is nice, but it does not last.

Then there is the third way—soaring. Only a few birds, like eagles, are capable of this. Eagles' wings are so strong that they are capable of catching rising currents of warm air—thermal winds that go straight up from the earth—and without moving a feather can soar up to great heights. Eagles have been clocked at up to 80 m.p.h. without flapping at all. They just soar on invisible columns of rising air.

Isaiah says that for those who wait on the Lord, times will come when they soar. You catch a gust of the spirit—Jesus said, "The wind blows wherever it pleases.... So it is with everyone born of the Spirit."

Sometimes in your life you will be in an era of spiritual soaring. Maybe you are there right now. You find yourself simply borne up by God's power. You are out of the boat. God is answering prayer with extravagant generosity, using you in ways that leave you astonished, giving you power to rise above temptation and sin, making you surprisingly productive in your life's work, and flooding you with strength and wisdom beyond your ability.

Be very grateful. Do all you can to stay in the stream of the Spirit's power—be very obedient as the Spirit guides you. Keep praying, and don't assume you are soaring on your own strength. Maybe there are particular disciplines helping you catch the Spirit's power—solitude, memorizing Scripture, simply getting enough rest. Identify these and be very diligent in them, build on them, and enjoy the ride. You are walking on the water. You are soaring with the Spirit.

But there is another line in Isaiah's description. Sometimes we are not soaring, but we are able to run and not grow weary. If this is where you are, your life isn't feeling effortless. You do not see a lot of miracles. You have to do some flapping. But with persistence and determination you know you are running the race. You feel frustration, but you also feel God's pleasure in your obedience. You need to keep running—faithfully obeying, serving, giving, and praying. Do not try to manufacture spiritual ecstasy. Do not compare yourself with someone who is soaring right now. Your time will come. Just keep running.

Then there is a third condition that Isaiah describes. Sometimes we will not be soaring, and we cannot run—because of doubt or pain or fatigue or failure. In those times all we can do is walk and not faint. This is not water-walking. It is just plain walking. All we can do is say, "God, I'll hang on. I don't seem too fruitful or productive, and I don't feel very triumphant. But I won't let go. I will obey you. I'll just keep walking."

One of the most powerful thirty minutes of film I have ever seen is the opening sequence of *Saving Private Ryan*. Veterans groups say it is perhaps the most realistic picture ever given of the brutal suffering the Allied soldiers faced on D-Day. An unbelievable price was paid to gain a toehold, a few feet of Omaha Beach in Normandy. It was paid in blood. At the end of D-Day, in one sense not much had changed. The vast majority of the continent of Europe was still, as it had been the day before, under the power of the swastika. There was just this one plot of ground, a few feet of sand on an obscure stretch of beach in one lonely country that was not under the domination of the enemy. But that one tiny stretch of land was enough.

The truth is, by the end of that one day, everything had changed. Now there was an opening. It was just a tiny crack, but it would get a little larger every day. The Allied forces would get a little stronger every day. There would still be a lot of fighting, a lot of suffering, a lot of dying. But now it was just a matter of time.

Until one day Paris was liberated. Then all of France. Nazi concentration camps were overrun. Prisoners were set free.

Then came the day when Hitler destroyed himself in the bunker. When judgment came to the beast, which it always does. Which it always will.

Then came V-E Day: Victory in Europe. Then V-J Day: Victory over Japan in the Pacific. The soldiers could come home. The war was over. The enemy was defeated.

Between the initial landing at Omaha Beach and the final firing of the final shot there was a long gap. But the truth is that victory was sealed on D-Day. After D-Day, V-E Day was just a matter of time.

One day a woman gave birth to a son, a male child, who was destined to rule all nations with a rod of iron. He taught about and lived in a kingdom, in a kind of life that the rest of us had always dreamed of, but hardly dared hope for.

I think that sometimes in Jesus' life—as when he was on the Mount of Transfiguration or when he called his friend Lazarus out of the tomb—Jesus soared. He rose so high in spirit that no one could keep up with him. He was in the jet stream.

At other times—as when he wept over the defiance of Jerusalem, when he was frustrated with the slowness of his disciples, when he faced the opposition of religious leaders—life was tougher. Yet he kept running. He did not turn aside from the course even when it ran uphill. He could run a long way.

But when it came time to take the road to Calvary, he wasn't soaring. When the cross was placed on his bruised and bleeding back, he wasn't running. He walked. He was a young man, but he stumbled and fell that day. All he could do was get back up and walk some more.

Sometimes walking is all we can do. But in those times, walking is enough. Maybe it is when life is the hardest, when we want so badly to quit, but we say to God, "I won't quit. I'll keep putting one foot in front of the other. I'll take up my cross. I'll follow Jesus even on this road." Maybe God prizes our walking even more than our soaring and our running.

Sometimes walking is all you can do. But in those times, walking is enough.

In any case, at a cost that none of us will ever fully understand, Jesus walked to Calvary. He took upon himself, on the cross, all the brokenness of the human race.

All the suffering of D-Day on Omaha Beach.

And all the suffering of all the sin and pain of every day of the history of human beings since the Fall.

After the Sabbath day, before Jesus' friends went to care for his body, the stone was dislocated—moved. In one sense nothing had changed. Pilate and the chief priests were still in charge; Caesar still reigned and didn't even know the name of this obscure Messiah in a remote country.

Nobody knew at first, except a couple of women, but that was D-Day. Now there was an opening. Tiny at first—no bigger than the entrance of a tomb.

Every time you engage in the battle, every time you resist sin, every time you proclaim the gospel, every time you give a portion of your resources for the spread of the kingdom, every time you offer a cup of cold water in Jesus' name, every time you "wait on the Lord"—every time, that opening gets a little larger. The darkness gets pushed back a little more. The light gets a little stronger.

We have some very fast runners in our world. We have some eagles that soar much higher than we can see. It is a hard thing to be a walker when you are surrounded by racers and eagles. But sometimes walking is the best we can offer God. He understands all about that. Walking counts, too.

> **What we wait for is not more important than what happens to us while we are waiting.**

And one day liberation will come. Make no mistake: There will still be a lot of fighting, a lot of suffering, a lot of dying. But D-Day has already happened—when hardly anyone was looking. At the end of that one day, everything had changed. So you keep walking, because what we wait for is not more important than what happens to us while we are waiting.

Now it is just a matter of time.

GETTING OUT OF THE BOAT

1. How do you tend to respond to waiting?
2. Why do you think Jesus waited so long to come to the disciples in the storm? In what ways have you seen waiting develop your character?
3. In what aspect of your life is waiting most difficult for you right now?
4. What would you say is the difference between "waiting on the Lord" versus "waiting around"? How might you transform your current waiting into "waiting on the Lord"?
5. Would you say that you are "soaring," "running," or "walking" these days?

CHAPTER 10

And those in the boat worshiped him, saying, "Truly you are the Son of God."

Matthew 14:33

How Big Is Your God?

Lord, help me to do great things as though they were little, since I do them with your power; and little things as though they were great, since I do them in your name.

Blaise Pascal

As soon as children are old enough to speak, one of the first questions parents ask is, "How big are you?"

Children always give the same answer, "I'm *soooo* big!" They generally raise their hands to get additional stature, as if to say, "I'm huge. I'm enormous. There's no telling how big I may be."

This is not a scientific answer. You can't use it in every context. For example, if your spouse were to ask, "How big do my hips look to you?" you might not want to throw your hands high over your head and exclaim, "Your hips are soooo big."

We teach our children to say this because we want them to realize they are growing. We know that the way they think of themselves matters. We don't want them to think of themselves as small, weak, and lacking adequate strength to handle the challenges of life.

But now I have a more important question: How big is your *God?* How big is Christ in your life?

Dale Bruner notes that right in the middle of the story of water-walking is the word that has the power to still the storms of fear in the troubled people of God: "Courage! I AM! Don't be afraid!" English translations usually add a word not found in the Greek: "I am *he*," or "It is I." But Matthew uses the Greek version of the great, mysterious, self-revealed name of God: "I AM WHO I AM"; "I AM has sent me to you."

As Bruner says, "This is no ordinary hello in water; it is the divine Lord addressing his needy church. The gospel of the story is in this great address." Jesus intends for his fear-prone followers to understand that this earth is in the hands of an infinite Lord whose character and competence can be trusted. "It's like this, dudes," he says. "Courage! I AM! Don't be afraid!"

I strongly believe that the way we live is a consequence of the size of our God. The problem many of us have is that our God is too small. We are not convinced that we are absolutely safe in the hands of a fully competent, all-knowing, ever-present God.

When we wake up in morning, what happens if we live with a small God?

We live in a constant state of fear and anxiety because everything depends on *us*. Our mood will be governed by our circumstances. We will live in a universe that leaves us deeply vulnerable.

When we have a chance to share our faith, we shrink back—what if we are rejected or cannot find the right words? It all depends on us.

We cannot be generous because our financial security depends on us.

When we need to give someone strong words of confrontation or challenge, we will be inclined to pull our punches. That is because if we don't live in the security of a big God's acceptance, we become slaves to what others think of us.

If we face the temptation to speak deceitful words to avoid pain, we will probably do it. We may try to get credit for something at work that does not belong to us because we don't trust in a Big God who sees in secret and will one day give reward.

If somebody gets mad at us or disapproves, we will get all twisted up in knots—we will not have the security of knowing that a giant God is watching out for us.

When human beings shrink God, they offer prayer without faith, work without passion, service without joy, suffering without hope. It results in fear, retreat, loss of vision, and failure to persevere.

How Big Is Jesus?

One day I was walking with a few friends in Newport Beach, California. We went past a bar where a fight that was going on inside spilled out onto the street, like a scene out of an old Western. Three men were beating up one lone opponent, and he was bleeding quite freely.

We had to do something, so we went over to break it up, to warn the aggressors in no uncertain terms that this fight was over. Unfortunately, I have not had much experience in that sort of thing. I missed the day that my seminary class covered how to break up barroom brawls. We had spent a little too much time in church to have effective language for that kind of intervention right at our fingertips. ("All right, you guys, cut it out right now! I'm serious!" works pretty well on three-year-olds in church who know you have access to their parents, but with seasoned gladiators who are running on sizable quantities of whiskey and testosterone, it is not so effective. Actually, it doesn't always work all that great on three-year-olds.)

Breaking up drunken brawls is not a strong area of spiritual passion or competence for me. But somebody had to do something, so we got out of the boat. We spoke prophetically to them, and then I waited for my first fistfight since I had been part of a church deacon board.

However, the thugs suddenly looked up at us with fear in their eyes and started to slink away. This caught me so much by surprise, I almost stopped them to ask why they were running away.

Then I looked behind me. There I saw one of the biggest guys I had ever seen. He was apparently employed as a bouncer at the barroom, and suddenly I gained a great deal of respect for that profession. I would guess the man stood about 6-foot-7 and weighed 250 pounds or so, with perhaps 2 percent body fat. If Hercules had married Xena the warrior princess, this could have been their child.

We called him Mongo. Not to his face, though.

"Mongo" did not say a word. He just stood there with muscles bulging. He looked as if he hoped they would try to take him on. This was an area of massive, breathtaking competence for him. Breaking up fights was his "spiritual gift."

In that moment, my attitude was transformed: "You'd better not let us catch you hanging around here again!" We were different people—*because we had a great big Mongo.*

I was ready to confront with resolve and firmness. I was filled with boldness and confidence. I was released from anxiety and fear. I was ready to serve someone who needed help.

Why? Because Mongo had passed by. I had experienced a Mongo-phany. I was convinced that I was not alone. The middle of a barroom brawl was a perfectly safe place for me to be.

If I were convinced that Mongo were with me twenty-four hours a day, seven days a week, I would have a fundamentally different approach to life.

Of course, he's not. I cannot go around with Mongo beside me all the time, and it is probably a good thing.

Because I don't need him.

I have One who is greater than Mongo with me at all times. "Courage!" he says. "I AM! Don't be afraid." I believe that. It is part of my creed. I have committed my life to teaching others about it. Yet all too often my life does not reflect it. All too often I shrink back when I should confront; I worry when I could pray; I cling when I could generously share; I stay in the boat when I could walk on the water.

So how can I change my perspective? How can I come to believe in the sufficiency of Christ for my life the way I now believe in grati-tude? How can I live in a way that reflects the fact that I follow a God who is *sooo big?*

There is a word for the process by which human beings come to perceive and declare the vastness, worthiness, and strength of God. It is called worship.

We live in a world that does not promote worship. Most of us are used to being measured by what we do. I know the lure of inde-pendence and self-sufficiency in deeply personal ways. And worship, on the surface of it, does not seem to be productive—it is not getting things *done.* So why do it? Let me explain why I have decided that I have to go through life as a worshiper. And let me make a case that you need to as well.

Why Does God Insist on Worship?

Have you ever wondered why God insists on being worshiped?

When my daughters were quite small, I would sometimes play a game with them in which I would ask, "Who's the smartest, strongest, wildest, most handsome, most charming, most attractive man in the whole world?"

They would be silent for several moments, as if giving the matter deep thought, then yell, "Santa Claus!" And then scream with laughter, as if they had just said the funniest thing in the world. As they got a little older, Santa Claus would be replaced by Big Bird, Mr. Rogers, Brad Pitt, or one of their mother's old boyfriends—whose numbers are legion. Eventually I gave up playing the game altogether.

My daughters were healthy enough to realize that you do not reinforce somebody's narcissistic ego needs by sitting around telling him how great he is.

So why does God insist on our worship? Does he really need to have a whole planet full of creatures spending vast amounts of effort and time dreaming up ways to tell him how great he is? Doesn't he already know that?

Worship is not about filling God's unmet ego needs. God has made us so that when we experience something transcendentally great, we have a need to praise it. Our experience is incomplete until we can wrap words around it. When we see the Grand Tetons for the first time, a double rainbow, or a nest of baby herons getting ready for their first flight, something in our spirits demands that we express the joy we receive.

(There is an old story about God telling Peter he was going to punish a golf-idolizing minister who skips church one Sunday and sneaks to a golf course instead. The old reverend smokes the course—the only below-par round of his life, topped off by his first and only hole-in-one on the eighteenth. Peter comments to God with some indignation: "I thought you said you were going to punish him." To which God replies: "I did. Who's he going to tell about it?")

When we see something profoundly admirable in another person, we don't just want to express it generally. Instead, our desire takes a new shape. For instance, if you are a single man, and you see a woman of great moral character, personal charm, and physical beauty— to whom do you want to express your admiration? (If you haven't answered "to her" by now, this may explain something about why you are still single.)

We are to worship God, not because his ego needs it, but because without worship, our experience and enjoyment of God are not complete. We worship God not so much because he needs it, but because *we* do.

I need to worship.

I need to worship because without it I can forget that I have a Big God beside me and live in fear. I need to worship because without it I can forget his calling and begin to live in a spirit of self-preoccupation. I need to worship because without it I lose a sense of wonder and gratitude and plod through life with blinders on. I need to worship because my natural tendency is toward self-reliance and stubborn independence.

I believe it is not an accident that the story of Peter walking on the water ends the way it does. "When they got into the boat, the wind ceased. And those in the boat worshiped him, saying, 'Truly you are the Son of God.'" There is a pattern at work here that recurs repeatedly in Scripture and that needs to become part of my life as well: God reveals himself. So we reflect on what God has done and respond in worship. And our understanding of God grows.

Jesus "passes by." This passing by may show itself in a highly dramatic way—a burning bush, a pillar of fire, a walk on the water. But often it happens in ways that are easily missed—in a still small voice, through a baby in an obscure manger. God may "pass by" for you in the comforting words of a friend, or in the beauty of a spring day when the earth begins to come back to life and you realize the heavens really "are telling the glory of God."

Then sometimes it will be in the act of getting out of the boat that I see Jesus passing by and I see a God who is bigger than I had imagined.

A friend and I were going to spend two weeks preaching in Ethiopia when it was still under Marxist rule. The underground churches that invited me over asked if we would bring fifty study Bibles with us. I had reservations about smuggling Bibles. But we decided to give it a shot. The churches we served donated the Bibles needed; in fact, just before we left, one woman came up and pressed an extra one in my hands, so we actually took fifty-one.

Sure enough, the customs agent opened one of the suitcases and confiscated the Bibles. A few days later we received a call that the head customs official wanted an interview with the leaders of the churches. We feared the worst—church leaders in Ethiopia spent so much time in prison they referred to it as "the university." (This is where God would send his leaders when he really wanted them to grow. Like the biblical Joseph, some of them would actually be put in charge by the guards when the guards wanted to go on break. They would take the bullets out of their rifles and hand them to the Christian prisoners to stand watch till they got back!) At best we were hoping we might be able to get the Bibles out of their hands through a bribe.

Imagine our surprise when the official said, "These Bibles are illegal. You may take them out on one condition—you must tell no one. I want to keep one for myself."

My God got a little larger that day. The Lord "intended to pass them by." Soooo big!

Every time someone gets out of the boat, their God gets a little bigger.

We Reflect on What God Has Done

Mark's version of the water-walking story says the disciples were amazed "because their hearts were hardened." They did not yet have eyes to see that in Jesus, *God had revealed himself*.

When I stop to reflect on what God has done, I seek to soften the hardness of my heart. Instead of walking through my day with blinders on, I *notice*.

Psychologists speak of a frequent human condition they call *mindlessness*. In mindlessness my body is present, but my mind is floating off somewhere else on auto pilot. Many of us suffer from mindlessness from time to time. For some of us it has become a way of life.

Let me give you an example. I will ask you a few questions, and you give the first answer that comes to mind. (Do it aloud if you are alone.)

—The tree that grows from an acorn is called an ....
—The vapor that rises from fire is called....
—The sound a frog makes is called a ....
—The white of an egg is called the ....

(If you didn't say "yolk," you are less mindless than I am.)

Sometimes mindlessness can infect a whole church. A writer in *The Christian Century* told about a congregation who had formatted all its services on computer. When a funeral service was to be held, they ran the same liturgy they had used for the last funeral, substituting only the name of the newly deceased (Edna) wherever the name of the previous woman (Mary) had been. On one occasion, everything proceeded smoothly until they came to the recitation of the Apostles' Creed, during which the people chanted together their belief in Jesus, "who was conceived of the Holy Spirit, born of the Virgin Edna...."

Mindlessness is one of the primary things that keeps us from worship. Ironically, we live in an age that seeks to eliminate mystery, and then we miss it. We have caller ID; we can know the gender of babies before they are born; exit polls tell us who was elected before we have finished voting; TV shows reveal the secrets magicians have always kept hidden—we destroy wonder and then ache for it.

But God is way too big for the wonder-killers. So we need to reflect a while.

We pause for a moment to consider the miracle called life that causes our lungs to keep sucking in air even without our remembering to give the orders, that causes our eyes to open in the morning so that we are resurrected each new day after the mini-death of sleep. What makes this happen?

We pause for a moment to consider the music when our child's voice comes through the telephone: "Dad!" These are just air molecules blowing into our ears in a configuration we have learned to recognize—but that one sound is so sweet that after fifteen years we never get tired of hearing it. How can air molecules beating on an eardrum produce such joy?

I watch, as I write these words, the pink-white blossoms of a crab apple tree on the shore before a rippling lake under an azure sky; my own private sea of Galilee. Just colors—light waves at some recognizable points on the photo-spectrum—but why do they make me so glad to be alive? Where does their beauty come from? The Lord "intended to pass them by...."

These are all miracles, all little theophanies crying out, "God lives! God cares! God is unspeakably good! God is sooo big!" to anyone not so mindless as to totally miss them.

Sometimes we miss these miracles because we are overwhelmed. But more often in my life it happens in retrospect. I see that God was at work in some way that I did not recognize at all at the time. More often I am like Jacob. "Then Jacob woke from his sleep and said, 'Surely the LORD is in this place—and I did not know it.'" We are seized by the *reality* of God.

We Respond in Worship

Responding in worship means more than just attending worship services on a regular basis. Sometimes, when I think of the "worship wars" of our day, I try to imagine similar arguments going on at the foot of Mount Sinai when the children had fled Egypt, the waters had parted into a temporary expressway, Pharaoh and his army had been drowned, the mountain was smoking and trembling, and the people were told to gather for worship.

—I don't like this worship. I liked that tambourine song that Miriam sang after we crossed the Red Sea. How come we don't do that song anymore?
—This service is too long. Three days is inconvenient. I'm going with the Hittites, they do two-day theophanies.
—I like it when Aaron leads worship. How come Moses has to be the worship leader? His vestments don't speak to my generation.

I suspect that when the Israelites gathered for worship, they trembled and shook along with the mountain because they had risked everything on this God—left home, food, and shelter. And he wanted to pass by.

I wonder occasionally if boredom in worship (and boredom in general) is not in fact a function of song selection or liturgical style, but rather, at least sometimes, a function of spending too much time in the boat. When we encounter this God, the Lord over mountains and storms, we tremble.

This brings us to the matter of "fearing God." The Bible says that "the fear of the LORD is the beginning of wisdom." Today we don't speak much of this. Our images of God have tended to grow smaller and more comfortable. Angels, for instance, have gone from awe-inspiring spiritual beings to comfortable personal guardians. C. S. Lewis noted that in Scripture, the appearance of an angel was always alarming; it had to begin every encounter by saying, "Fear not." But a Victorian angel always looks as if it were going to say, "There, there. Easy now."

What does it mean to fear the Lord?

We have no need to be afraid that God will do mean or destructive things. We do not need to be afraid that God's love is not fully trustworthy. Cold Comfort Farm, an English film, featured a sect called "the quivering brethren," who constantly shook from their fear of God. Their favorite hymn ended with the words, "The world will burn, but we will quiver."

When the Bible says that "the fear of the LORD is the beginning of wisdom," it does not call us to be quivering brethren. One of C. S. Lewis's characters expresses fear at the prospect of meeting his Christ-figure, the great lion Aslan, and wonders if he is quite safe. "Safe? Who said anything about safe. Of course he's not safe. But he's good."

This fear involves reverence and awe, a healthy recognition of who God is. It also involves a recognition of our fallenness. Remember the definition of fear that we looked at in chapter 6: Fear is designed to call attention to danger so we can set things right.

But worship also reminds me that the day will come when our fallenness will be utterly healed. In that day we will fully realize the truth of the saying that "perfect love casts out fear." When we worship, we look forward to the day when fear will be as defeated and destroyed as sin, guilt, and death. Worship, therefore, in reminding us of this powerful God who is for us, becomes one of the great weapons against fear.

Dallas Willard writes,

> Holy delight and joy is the great antidote to despair and is a wellspring of genuine gratitude—the kind that starts at our toes and blasts off from our loins and diaphragm through the top of our head, flinging our arms and our eyes and our voice upward toward our good God.

It may be that such worship comes quite naturally to you. That was not the case for me. I grew up in the Swedish Baptist church, and Swedes are not naturally expressive, chandelier-swinging worshipers. A Swedish extrovert is someone who looks down at *your* shoes when talking to you. When Swedes get worked up into an emotional lather, you can tell because they will say things like "Yaaah, suuuure, you betcha big fellah." And they will remember an ecstatic outburst like that for years.

I had to learn to respond.

Max DePree said that the first task of a leader is to define reality. God, being the ultimate Leader, takes that task quite seriously. And worship fundamentally is about the definition of reality.

Now, in worship I use every tool at my disposal—memory, imagination, music, Scripture, images, pictures, and dance—to magnify God in my life. In worship I declare that God is real. In worship my perception of reality is changed and sharpened. In worship I remember that reality is more than what I can see and touch. In worship I acknowledge that I look at a shrunken God on a regular basis, looking at him through the wrong end of the telescope.

Worship fundamentally is about the definition of reality.

So in worship, at its heart, we *magnify* God. One of the Greek words for worship begins with the prefix *mega*, meaning large, which gets attached in our day to everything from malls to churches. In worship I remember again that we worship the great God, the Mega God, the Lord of lords. In one of the classic songs of worship in the New

Testament, Mary cries out, "My soul *magnifies* the Lord." Worship enlarges my capacity to experience and understand God.

In C. S. Lewis's *Prince Caspian,* one of the children comes upon Aslan, the Christ-figure of the Narnia stories, after a prolonged absence. "Aslan, you're bigger," she says.

"That is because you're older, little one," answered he.

"Not because you are?"

"I am not. But every year you grow, you will find me bigger."

So it is with us and God. This is why the story of Peter walking on the water *must* end in worship. Worship, in a sense, closes the loop on the whole story. Worship consolidates and expresses the disciples' new understanding of who Jesus is.

Peter gets into the boat, and the other disciples ask him, "How big is Jesus, anyway?"

Peter throws his hands up high over his head and says, "Jesus is *sooo* big!"

Jesus gets into the boat, the wind dies down, the storm runs away to wherever it is storms go when God sends them off, and suddenly the disciples have a deeper understanding of who is in the boat with them. "Truly you are the Son of God."

And all the disciples raise their hands up over their heads.

Soooo big!

So it always is when somebody gets out of the boat. When human beings get out of the boat, they are never quite the same. Their worship is never quite the same. Their world is never quite the same. Whatever the results, whether they sink or swim, something will have changed.

> Jesus is not finished yet. He is still looking for people who will dare to trust him.

This is true for you. From this point on, for the rest of your life, every time you walk on the water, each time you trust God and seek to discern and obey his calling on your life, your God will get bigger, and your worship will grow deeper, richer, and stronger.

That is because Jesus is not finished yet. He is still looking for people who will dare to trust him. He is still looking for people who will refuse to allow fear to have the final word. He is still looking for people who refuse to be deterred by failure. He is still passing by. And this is your one and only opportunity to answer his call.

This is your chance of a lifetime.

It is time to do something religious.

Just remember one thing: If you want to walk on the water, you've got to get out of the boat.

GETTING OUT OF THE BOAT

1. How would you characterize your worship at this time?
2. When in your life did you most find your understanding of God getting bigger? What prompted this?
3. Is God getting bigger to you right now, or smaller, or staying the same?
4. What step could you take to "magnify God" in your life?
5. If your God truly is a big God, and you could ask him to do any one thing in your life, what would it be?

Sources

All italics in quotations have been added by the author and are not in the original unless otherwise noted. Scripture quotations are from the *New Revised Standard Version* unless indicated otherwise.

Chapter 1: On Water-Walking

11: *Roosevelt:* Theodore Roosevelt, "Citizenship in a Republic," speech at the Sorbonne, Paris, April 23, 1910.

14: *"Tormented" by the waves:* Matthew 14:24 as rendered in F. D. Bruner, *Matthew*, vol. 2, Word Biblical Commentary. Dallas: Word Books, 1985, 532.

14: *Garland:* David E. Garland, *NIV Application Commentary: Mark.* Grand Rapids: Zondervan, 1996, 263.

14: *"Intended to pass them by":* Mark 6:48–49.

15: *"While my glory passes by":* Exodus 33:22; 34:6.

15: *"The LORD is about to pass by":* 1 Kings 19:11.

15: *"He alone . . . treads":* Job 9:8 NIV.

15: *Bruner: Matthew,* 2:533.

16: *"If it is you, command me":* Matthew 14:28.

20: *Guder:* Quoted in Bill and Kathy Peel, *Discover Your Destiny.* Colorado Springs: NavPress, 1996, 25.

20: *Laudan:* Larry Laudan, *Danger Ahead.* New York: John Wiley & Sons, 1997, 3.

21: *Jeffers:* Susan Jeffers, *Feel the Fear and Do It Anyway.* New York: Fawcett Columbine, 1987, 22.

24: *"You of little faith":* Matthew 14:31.

26: *"Even youths will faint":* Isaiah 40: 30–31.

Chapter 2: Boat Potatoes

31: *Dante:* Dante Alighieri, *The Divine Comedy,* "Inferno," Canto 3, 35–38.

33: *Bruner:* F. D. Bruner, *Matthew*, vol. 2, Word Biblical Commentary. Dallas: Word Books, 1985, 535.

34: *Levoy:* Gregg Levoy, *Callings: Finding and Following an Authentic Life.* New York: Crown Publishers, 1997, 9.

35: *Keillor:* Garrison Keillor, *Lake Wobegon Days.* New York: Penguin Books, 1985, 413–14.

36: *Thoreau:* Henry David Thoreau, *Walden,* in *The Portable Thoreau.* New York: Viking Press, 1947, 344.

37: *Bailey:* Kenneth E. Bailey, *Poet and Peasant: Through Peasant's Eyes.* Grand Rapids: Wm. B. Eerdmans, 1983, 167.

41: *Jeffers:* Susan Jeffers, *Feel the Fear and Do It Anyway.* New York: Fawcett Columbine, 1987.

45: *Schimmel:* Solomon Schimmel, *The Seven Deadly Sins. New York:* Oxford University Press, 1997, 193.

46: *DePree:* Max DePree, *Leadership Is an Art.* New York: Dell Books, 1990, 5.

48: *St. Jerome:* Bruner, *Matthew.*

48: *"You have been trustworthy"*: Matthew 25:21, 23.

49: *"To the one who conquers"*: Revelation 3:21.

51: *"Beloved, we are God's children"*: 1 John 3:2.

Chapter 3: Discerning the Call

53: *Buber:* Martin Buber, quoted by Gregg Levoy, *Callings: Finding and Following an Authentic Life.* New York: Harmony Books, 1997, 2.

53: *Calvin and Chrysostom:* Quoted in F. D. Bruner, *Matthew,* vol. 2, Word Biblical Commentary. Dallas: Word Books, 1985, 535.

55: *Keillor:* Garrison Keillor, *Lake Wobegon Days.* New York: Penguin Books, 1985, 413–14.

57: *Ryken:* Leland Ryken, *Work and Leisure.* Portland, OR: Multnomah Press, 1987.

57: *"You make springs gush forth"*: Psalm 104:10, 13, 14, 24.

57: *"My Father is still working"*: John 5:17.

57: *Minear:* Paul Minear, "Work and Vocation in Scripture," in *Work and Vocation: A Christian Discussion,* ed. John Oliver Nelson. New York: Harper Brothers, 1954, 44.

57: *"The* LORD *God formed man"*: Genesis 2:7.

58: *Miller:* Arthur F. Miller Jr., *The Power of Uniqueness.* Grand Rapids: Zondervan, 1999, 21.

60: *Novak:* Michael Novak, *Business as a Calling.* New York: Simon and Schuster, 1996, 18, 38.

60: *Palmer:* Parker Palmer, *Let Your Life Speak.* San Francisco: Jossey-Bass, 2000, 15.

60: *Buechner:* Frederich Buechner, *Wishful Thinking.* San Francisco: HarperSan Francisco, 1993, 119.

61: *Miller: The Power of Uniqueness,* 40.

61: *"In the heavens he has set a tent":* Psalm 19:4–5.

62: *Palmer: Let Your Life Speak,* 16.

64: *Csikszentmihalyi:* Mihaly Csikszentmihalyi, *Flow: The Psychology of Optimal Experience.* New York: HarperCollins, 1990, 157.

64: *McFeely:* William McFeely, *Grant: A Biography.* New York: W. W. Norton, 1981, 242–43.

66: *Palmer: Let Your Life Speak,* 39.

67: *"Sober judgment":* Romans 12:3.

67: *Buford:* Bob Buford, *Halftime: Changing Your Game Plan from Success to Significance.* Grand Rapids: Zondervan, 1994, 100.

68: *Miller: The Power of Uniqueness,* 115.

69: *Smith:* Gordon Smith, *In Times of Choice.* Downers Grove, IL: InterVarsity Press, 1997.

70: *Blackaby:* Henry Blackaby, *Experiencing God.* Nashville: Broadman & Holman, 1994.

71: *Hunnicutt:* Benjamin Kline Hunnicutt, *Work Without End: Abandoning Shorter Hours for the Right to Work.* Philadelphia: Temple University Press, 1988.

72: *Colson:* Quoted in David Ireland, *Failure Is Written in Pencil.* Old Greenwich, CT: Impact Publishing, 2000, 40.

Chapter 4: Walking on the Water

75: *Thoreau:* Henry David Thoreau, *Walden,* in *The Portable Thoreau.* New York: Viking Press, 1947, 343.

78: *God makes the earth tremble:* See Psalm 104:32.

78: *He raises his voice:* See Psalm 46:6.

78: *"Peace! Be still!":* Mark 4:39.

79: *"Be strong and courageous":* Joshua 1:9.

79: *"When the soles of the feet":* Joshua 3:13.

81: *Luther:* Theodore Tappert, ed. and trans., *Luther's Works,* vol. 54, American ed. Philadelphia: Fortress Press, 1967, 453.

82: *Hallesby:* Ole Hallesby, *Prayer.* N.d.

82: *"Without faith it is impossible":* Hebrews 11:6.

84: *Diagram:* Adapted from a concept of Susan Jeffers, *Feel the Fear and Do It Anyway*. New York: Fawcett Columbine, 1987, 44.

85: *Cotter:* Jeffrey Cotter, "Witness Upmanship," *Eternity*, March 1981, 22–23.

Chapter 5: Seeing the Wind

95: *Levoy:* Gregg Levoy, *Callings: Finding and Following an Authentic Life*. New York: Crown Publishers, 1997, 253.

95: *Ambrose:* Stephen Ambrose, *Undaunted Courage: Meriwether Lewis, Thomas Jefferson, and the Opening of the American West*. New York: Simon & Schuster/Touchstone, 1997.

99: *"Coat of many colors":* Genesis 37:3 KJV.

100: *"So they hated him even more":* Genesis 37:8.

102: *"But Daniel resolved":* Daniel 1:8.

102: *Peter and the other apostles:* See Acts 4, especially vv. 18–21.

102: *"About midnight Paul and Silas":* Acts 16:25.

103: *"Joseph found favor":* Genesis 39:4, 6.

103: *Abba Anthony:* Quoted in Robert Roberts, *The Strengths of a Christian*. Philadelphia: Westminster Press, 1984, 56.

105: *"And although she spoke to Joseph":* Genesis 39:10.

105: *"One day . . . she caught hold of his garment":* Genesis 39:11–12.

106: *Jung:* Carl Jung, *Collected Works of C. G. Jung*, vol. 2. Princeton, NJ: Princeton University Press, 1973, 75.

108: *"The LORD was with Joseph":* Genesis 39:21.

108: *Frankl:* Victor Frankl, *Man's Search for Meaning*. New York: Washington Square, 1963.

109: *Szymusik:* cited in Julius Segal, "Possible Interventions with Risk-Prone Individuals," in *Self-Regulating Behavior and Risk Taking*, ed. Lewis Lipsitt and Leonard Mitnick. Norwood, NJ: Ablex Publishing, 1991, 334.

109: *"Tired of Life":* E. Schneidman and N. Farberow, "A Psychological Approach to the Study of Suicide Notes" in *The Psychology of Suicide*, ed. E. Schneidman, N. Farberow, and R. Litman. New York: Science House, 1970, 159–64.

109: *Segal:* "Possible Interventions," 334.

109: *Garland:* David E. Garland, *NIV Application Commentary: Mark*. Grand Rapids: Zondervan, 1996, 263.

109: *"The LORD was with Joseph":* Genesis 39:21–22.

111: *Peck:* M. Scott Peck, *The Road Less Traveled.* New York: Simon & Schuster, 1978, 16.

111: *Weiner:* David Weiner, *Battling the Inner Dummy.* Amherst, NY: Prometheus Books, 1999, 301.

112: *"Within three days Pharaoh will lift up your head":* Genesis 40:13.

112: *"Within three days Pharaoh will lift up your head—from you!":* Genesis 40:19.

113: *"Even though you intended to do harm to me":* Genesis 50:20.

114: *Willard:* Dallas Willard, *The Divine Conspiracy.* San Francisco: HarperSanFrancisco, 1999, 237.

Chapter 6: Crying Out in Fear

117: *Thoreau:* Henry David Thoreau, journal entry, September 7, 1851.

118: *Ogilvie:* Lloyd Ogilvie, *Facing the Future Without Fear.* Ann Arbor: Vine Books, 1999, 22.

119: *Bruner:* F. D. Bruner, *Matthew,* vol. 2, Word Biblical Commentary. Dallas: Word Books, 1985, 534, including Scripture quotations.

122: *Dozier:* Rush Dozier, *Fear Itself.* New York: St. Martin's Press, 1998, 10ff.

123: *Le Doux:* Edward Hallowell, *Worry.* New York: Ballantine Books, 1997, xiv.

123: *Gene slc6a4:* Stephen Hall, "The Anatomy of Fear," *New York Times Magazine,* February 28, 1999, 45.

124: *Jeffers:* Susan Jeffers, *Feel the Fear and Do it Anyway.* New York: Ballantine Books, 1987.

124: *American Psychological Association:* Richard Bednar and Scott Peterson, *Self-Esteem: Paradoxes and Innovations in Clinical Theory and Practice.* Washington, DC: American Psychological Association, 1995.

132: *Sweet:* Leonard Sweet, *A Cup of Coffee at the Soul Café.* Nashville: Broadman & Holman, 1998, 130.

133: *"As for mortals, their days are like grass":* Psalm 103:15–16.

Chapter 7: That Sinking Feeling

135: *Melville:* Quoted in William McFeely, *Grant: A Biography.* New York: W. W. Norton, 1981, 485.

136: *Bruner:* F. D. Bruner, *Matthew,* vol. 2, Word Biblical Commentary. Dallas: Word Books, 1985, 535.

136: *Goleman:* Daniel Goleman, *Emotional Intelligence.* New York: Bantam Books, 1995, 80.

138: *"Very much afraid of Achish king of Gath":* 1 Samuel 21:12–15.

138: *"David left [Gath]":* 1 Samuel 22:1.

139: *"Everyone who was in distress":* 1 Samuel 22:2.

139: *"Until they had no more strength":* 1 Samuel 30:4.

140: *"David was in great danger":* 1 Samuel 30:6.

140: *"With my voice I cry to the LORD":* Psalm 142:1–2.

142: *"It is enough . . . take away my life:* 1 Kings 19:4.

142: *An angel bake him a cake:* See 1 Kings 19:6.

143: *"You are my refuge":* Psalm 142:5.

143: *"Pursue; for you shall surely overtake":* 1 Samuel 30:8.

144: *Burns:* David Burns, *Feeling Good.* New York: William Morrow, 1980, 80ff.

144: *Warren:* Neil Clark Warren, *Finding the Love of Your Life: Ten Principles for Choosing the Right Marriage Partner.* New York: Pocket Books, 1994.

145: *Brim:* Gilbert Brim, *Ambition: How We Manage Success and Failure Throughout Our Lives.* New York: HarperCollins, 1992, 77.

145: *Palmer:* Parker Palmer, *Let Your Life Speak.* San Francisco: Jossey-Bass, 2000. Used by permission.

148: *Art and Fear:* David Bayles and Ted Orland, *Art and Fear: Observations on the Perils (and Rewards) of Artmaking.* Santa Barbara: Capra Press, 1993, 29.

148: *"He came to the sheepfolds":* 1 Samuel 24:3.

149: *Miller:* Arthur Miller, *Death of a Salesman.* New York: Penguin Books, 1949, 110–11.

150: *"You are my refuge":* Psalm 142:5.

Chapter 8: Focusing on Jesus

153: *Seligman:* Martin Seligman, *Learned Optimism.* New York: Simon & Schuster, 1990, 16.

156: *Smedes:* Lewis B. Smedes, *Standing on the Promises.* Nashville: Thomas Nelson 1998, 28.

157: *Moses sent out twelve scouts:* See Numbers 13.

158: *Seligman: Learned Optimism,* 15.

159: *Goleman:* Daniel Goleman, *Emotional Intelligence.* New York: Bantam Books, 1995, 87.

159: *In one study, 122 men:* Chris Peterson, "Optimism and By-pass Surgery," in *Learned Helplessness: A Theory for the Age of Personal Control.* New York: Oxford University Press, 1993.

159: *MacDonald:* Gordon MacDonald, *Mid-Course Correction.* Nashville: Thomas Nelson, 2000, ix.

160: *Lasch:* Christopher Lasch, *The True and Only Heaven.* New York: W. W. Norton, 1991, 81.

160: *"I can do all things":* Philippians 4:13.

161: *"Whatever is true":* Philippians 4:8.

161: *Hart:* Archibald Hart, *Habits of the Mind.* Dallas: Word, 1996, 5.

162: *"Do not be conformed to this world":* Romans 12:2.

163: *"Thou wilt keep him in perfect peace":* Isaiah 26:3 KJV.

164: *Laubach:* Laubach Literary International, *Frank Laubach: Man of Prayer.* Syracuse: Laubach Literacy International, 1990, 78.

167: *"May the God of hope fill you":* Romans 15:13 NIV.

168: *Psychologists tell us:* Evan Imber-Black and Janine Roberts, *Rituals for Our Times.* Northvale, NJ: Aronson, 1998.

Chapter 9: Learning to Wait

173: *Smedes:* Lewis B. Smedes, *Standing on the Promises.* Nashville: Thomas Nelson 1998.

173: *Levine:* Robert Levine, *A Geography of Time.* New York: Basic Books, 1997, 152.

174: *"During the fourth watch of the night":* Matthew 14:25 NIV.

174: *Rawlinson:* A. E. J. Rawlinson, *St. Mark,* Westminster Commentaries. London: Methuen, 1925, 88.

176: *Mouw:* Richard Mouw, *Uncommon Decency.* Downers Grove, IL: InterVarsity Press, 1992, 159.

176: *Smedes: Standing on the Promises,* 41–42.

177: *"Be still before the* LORD*":* Psalm 37:7, 34.

177: *"Was righteous and devout":* Luke 2:25 NIV.

177: *"Do not leave Jerusalem":* Acts 1:4 NIV.

177: *"We ourselves ... groan inwardly":* Romans 8:23–25.

178: *"The one ... says, 'Surely I am coming soon'":* Revelation 22:20.

178: *Peck:* M. Scott Peck, *The Road Less Traveled.* New York: Simon & Schuster, 1978, 19.

178: *Goleman:* Daniel Goleman, *Emotional Intelligence.* New York: Bantam Books, 1995.

179: *Goleman: Emotional Intelligence*, 80.

180: *"But do not ignore this one fact"*: 2 Peter 3:8.

182: *Nouwen:* Henri M. J. Nouwen, *Sabbatical Journey: The Diary of His Final Year*. New York: Crossroad Publishing, 1998, 2ff.

182: *"The effect of righteousness will be peace"*: Isaiah 32:17.

184: *"For in hope we were saved"*: Romans 8:24–25.

184: *Hoffmann:* Ernst Hoffmann, "Hope," *Dictionary of New Testament Theology*, vol. 2, ed. Colin Brown. Grand Rapids: Zondervan, 1978, 243ff.

184: *"Even youths will faint and be weary"*: Isaiah 40:30–31.

186: *"The wind blows wherever it pleases"*: John 3:8 NIV.

Chapter 10: How Big Is Your God?

191: *Pascal:* Quoted in Bill and Kathy Peel, *Discover Your Destiny*. Colorado Springs: NavPress, 1996, 215.

192: *Bruner:* F. D. Bruner, *Matthew*, vol. 2, Word Biblical Commentary. Dallas: Word Books, 1985, 534.

196: *"When they got into the boat"*: Matthew 14:32–33.

199: *"Then Jacob woke from his sleep"*: Genesis 28:16.

200: *"The fear of the LORD"*: Proverbs 9:10.

200: *"Perfect love casts out fear"*: 1 John 4:18.

201: *Willard:* Dallas Willard, *The Spirit of the Disciplines*. San Francisco: HarperSanFrancisco, 1988, 178.

201: *DePree:* Max DePree, *Leadership Is an Art*. New York: Dell Books, 1990, 5f.

202: *Lewis:* C. S. Lewis, *Prince Caspian*, The Chronicles of Narnia. New York: Collier/Macmillan, 1985, 136.

Read an excerpt from

BESTSELLING AUTHOR

JOHN ORTBERG

FOREWORD BY DR. HENRY CLOUD

SOUL
KEEPING

CARING *for* THE MOST IMPORTANT
PART *of* YOU

CHAPTER 1

THE SOUL NOBODY KNOWS

One of the most important words in the Bible is *soul*. We throw that word around a lot, but if someone were to ask you to explain exactly what the word *soul* means, what would you say?

- *Why should I pay attention to my soul?*
- *Hasn't science disproven its existence?*
- *Isn't the soul the province of robe-wearing, herbal-tea drinkers?*
- *Isn't "soul-saving" old-fashioned language that ignores concerns for holistic justice?*
- *Won't it mean preoccupation with navel-gazing? Will I have to go to Big Sur or look at some stranger in the eyes? Will I have to journal?*

Belief in the soul is ubiquitous: "Most people, at most times, in most places, at most ages, have believed that human beings have some kind of souls." We know it matters. We suspect it's important. But we're not sure what it means.

It's the word that won't go away, even though it is used less and less.

From birth to our final resting place ("May God rest his soul"), the soul is our earliest companion and our ultimate concern. The word is ethereal, mysterious, and deep. And a little spooky. ("All Souls' Day" comes two days after Halloween and has always sounded to me like disembodied spirits floating around at the Haunted Mansion in Disneyland.)

How many of our children learned this prayer? How many times have *you* recited it at bedtime?

> Now I lay me down to sleep,
> I pray the Lord my soul to keep.
> If I should die before I wake,
> I pray the Lord my soul to take.

What does it mean to ask God "my soul to keep"? If I expire before sunrise, and he takes my soul, what exactly is it that gets taken?

HOW MUCH DOES A SOUL WEIGH?

Jeffrey Boyd is a kind of Don Quixote of the soul. He is a Yale psychiatrist, an ordained minister, and coauthor of *Diagnostic and Statistical Manual of Mental Disorders*, a work in which you will search in vain for a single reference to "soul." It does include something called "depersonalization disorder," a feeling of estrangement from oneself. But Boyd also writes books and articles trying to reinject the word *soul* into our scientific vocabulary.

In one study of hundreds of church attenders, Boyd found that most people believe they know what *soul* means, but when asked to explain it, they can't do it. The soul turns out to be like Supreme Court Justice Potter Stewart's description of obscenity: "It may be hard to define, but I know it when I see it." About half of church attenders adopt what Boyd calls the Looney Tunes Theory of the soul:

> If Daffy Duck were blown up with dynamite, then there would be a transparent image of Daffy Duck that would float up from the dead body. The translucent image would have wings and carry a harp. From the air this apparition would speak down to Bugs Bunny, who set off the dynamite.

It sounds funny to talk about cartoons when it comes to the soul, but as Aristotle said, "The soul never thinks without a picture."

The soul can't be put under a microscope or studied by X-ray. About a hundred years ago a doctor measured the slight weight loss experienced by seven tuberculosis victims at the moment of death, which led him to claim that the soul weighs twenty-one grams. His idea years later created a title for a movie with Sean Penn and Naomi Watts, but it was never duplicated and was widely ridiculed in the medical community. Some are convinced that soul language needs to go.

A philosopher named Owen Flanagan says there is no place in science for the notion of a soul: "Desouling is the primary operation of the scientific image."

But Boyd argues that we see people who have a strength of soul that simply will not be degraded by the humiliation their body puts them through.... The soul knows a glory that the body cannot rob. In some ways, in some cases, the more the body revolts, the more the soul shines through.

THE HIGH AND THE LOW
OF THE SOUL

We can't seem to talk about beauty or art without talking about the soul—particularly music. Aretha Franklin is the Queen of Soul. It is possible that if your soul isn't moved by Ray Charles, Otis Redding, Little Richard, Fats Domino, or James Brown, you may want to check to make sure you still have one. Kid Rock wrote "Rebel Soul." A sixteen-year-old, wanna-be pop singer named Jewel hitchhiked to Mexico and watched desperate people looking for help and wrote what would become her breakthrough song: "Who Will Save Your Soul?"

We need the word when we speak of not just the highest, but also the lowest parts of human existence. Over one hundred years ago, W.E.B. Du Bois called his book about the oppressed humanity of a race *The Souls of Black Folk*. No other word would do: *The Selves of Black Folk* does not carry the same dignity. "Soul food" would be the name given for southern cooking that began with slaves who had to survive on whatever leftovers they were given. "Soul power" became the name for a sense of dignity and worth in a people who had been forced to live with none. "Soul brother" reflects the bond that knits together those persecuted because of skin color.

Does soul require suffering to make itself known?

We speak of larger entities having soul. During every election, politicians and pundits warn us that the soul of America is at stake. ServiceMaster CEO William Pollard wrote a leadership book called *The Soul of the Firm.* Shortstop and team captain Derek Jeter has been given the title "soul of the Yankees." Quarterback Tom Brady deemed receiver Wes Walker the "soul" of the New England Patriots. These may be metaphors, but they point to the notion of the soul as that which holds a larger entity together.

SOUL FOR SALE

We speak of the soul as a source of strength, and yet we speak of it as fragile. Something about the soul always seems to be at risk. A soul is something that can be lost or sold. The selling of a soul has been made into countless operas, books, and country music lyrics, as well as a movie called *Bedazzled* and a musical called *Damn Yankees....* In the television series *The Simpsons*, Homer sells his soul for a donut and then impulsively eats all but one bite, which he puts in the refrigerator with the instructions: "Soul Donut. Do Not Eat." ...

Does a fetus have a soul? A whole debate about abortion rages around this one. Does life happen at conception? Is that when a being becomes human? Plato believed that souls were reincarnated based on how elevated they had been last time around: wise souls come back as seekers of beauty or kings or athletic trainers, whereas cowards come back as women and boozers may come back as donkeys. Augustine said that maybe souls preexist somewhere and then slip into bodies on their own, like people picking out a good car.

We are not sure what the soul is, but the word sells. Advertisers speak of cars being soulful; Kia actually manufactures a car called the Kia Soul. Is it for people who want to go beyond transportation to transmigration? You can also find the Soul Diva (for the "style conscious woman who regards her car as important as her entire outfit");

the Soul Burner (the "bad boy" of the Soul concept); and the Soul Searcher (for the driver focused on "achieving personal inner peace and creating a calm cocoon for occupants").

The word *soul* won't go away, because it speaks somehow of eternity:

> Now there are some things we all know, but we don't take'em out and look at'm very often. We all know that *something* is eternal. And it ain't houses and it ain't names and it ain't earth, and it ain't even the stars.... everybody knows in their bones that *something* is eternal, and that something has to do with human beings. All the greatest people ever lived have been telling us that for five thousand years and yet you'd be surprised how people are always losing hold of it....

A WINDOW TO YOUR SOUL

We speak of the eyes being the window to the soul. Scientists say the eyes can reveal our inner thoughts. For instance, when people are doing hard mental work, their pupils dilate. Daniel Kahneman wrote about researchers monitoring the eyes of subjects trying to solve difficult math problems. They would sometimes surprise subjects by asking them, "Why did you give up just now?"

"How did you know?" the unsuspecting students asked.

"We have a window to your soul."

Psychologist Edmund Hess writes how pupils widen when people look at beautiful nature pictures. When I was in grad school, I saw two famous pictures of a lovely woman — identical, except that in one of them, her pupils are dilated, and that picture is always judged much more attractive. Belladonna, an herb-based drug that expands the pupils, is actually sold as a cosmetic. Professional poker players sometimes wear sunglasses simply to keep their pupils from giving their excitement away.

U.S. President George W. Bush said that when he looked into Russian President Vladimir Putin's eyes, he was able to get a sense of his soul....

When we talk of love, we speak of soul. No one searches for the love of their life on a site called BodyMate.com. In his dialogue *The Symposium*, Plato has Aristophanes present the story of soul mates. Aristophanes states that humans originally had four arms, four legs, and a single head made of two faces, but Zeus feared their power and split them all in half, condemning them to spend their lives searching for the other half to complete them. In the film *Jerry Maguire*, Tom Cruise's character expresses the idea unforgettably to Renée Zellweger: "You complete me." Can one person really complete another? Do we all have one and only one soul mate out there in the world someplace?

Churches are supposed to know about souls. We often sing a song that originated as a psalm: "Bless the Lord, O My Soul." How can your soul bless, or make happy, the Lord? Sometimes we speak of souls as if they are spiritual scalps: certain people who are highly regarded as "soul-winners" or who are especially adept at going after "lost souls." We get teary-eyed at the evangelist who desires to win "just one more soul for Jesus." Old-time evangelist Billy Sunday used to calculate how much money it cost him to save a soul: in Boston in 1911 it was $450. Churches did the job more economically: Congregationalists came in at $70 per soul, Baptists at $70, and Methodists at a staggeringly low $3.12 — which was cheap even by the 1911 standards!

The universal distress signal, SOS, is said to stand for "Save Our Souls." What does it mean for a soul to be saved?

"I don't deserve a soul, yet I still have one," writes Douglas Coupland. "I know because it hurts." ...

We search for the soul because we're curious. But not just that. The search for the soul always begins with our great hurt.

If I should die before I wake, I pray the Lord my soul to take ...
What is the soul?

SOURCES

"Most people, at most times": Mark Baker and Stewart Goetz, *The Soul Hypothesis* (New York: Continuum Books, 2011), 100.

"If Daffy Duck were": Jeffrey Boyd, *Soul Psychology* (Colorado Springs: Soul Research Institute, 1994), 59.

Soul weighs twenty-one grams: Les Parrott, *You're Stronger Than You Think* (Carol Stream, IL: Tyndale, 2012), 116.

Owen Flanagan: Baker and Goetz, *The Soul Hypothesis,* 100.

William Pollard, *The Soul of the Firm* (Grand Rapids: Zondervan, 2000).

W.E.B Du Bois, *The Souls of Black Folk* (Healdburg, CA: Eucalyptus Press, 2013).

Plato believed that souls were re-incarnated: Steward Goetz and Charles Taliaferro, *A Brief History of the Soul* (Malden, MA: Wiley-Blackwell, 2011), 12.

Augustine said that maybe souls preexist: Ibid., 44 – 45.

"Now there are some things": Thornton Wilder, *Our Town* (New York: Harper & Row, 1938), 87 – 88.

Edmund Hess: cited in Daniel Kahneman, *Thinking Fast and Slow* (New York: Farrar, Straus, and Giroux, 2011), 32.

"soulful work" movement: www.soulfulwork.net

cost to save soul: *The New York Times* (October 9, 1911), section 7.

"I don't deserve a soul": Douglas Coupland, *The Gum Thief* (New York: Bloomsbury, 2007), 21.

"If a child is born": Jeffrey Boyd, "One's Self-Concept and Biblical Theology," *Journal of the Evangelical Theological Society* 40:2 (June 1997): 223.

Soul Keeping

Caring for the Most Important Part of You

Bestselling Author John Ortberg

The soul is NOT "a theological and abstract subject."

The soul is the coolest, eeriest, most mysterious, evocative, crucial, sacred, eternal, life-directing, fragile, indestructible, controversial, expensive dimension of your existence.

Jesus said it's worth more than the world.

You'd be an idiot not to prize it above all else.

Shouldn't you get pretty clear on exactly what it is? Shouldn't you know what it runs on? Wouldn't it be worth knowing how to care for it?

Two things are for sure. One is: you have a soul. The other is: if you don't look after this one, you won't be issued a replacement.

Bestselling author John Ortberg writes another classic that will help readers discover their soul and take their relationship with God to the next level.

Available in stores and online!

ZONDERVAN®
.com

Soul Keeping
Study Guide and DVD
Caring for the Most Important Part of You

Bestselling Author John Ortberg

In this six-session, video-based small group Bible study, Ortberg shows that caring for your soul is necessary for your Christian life. John shows participants what your soul is, why it is important, how to assess your soul's health, and how to care for it so that we can have a meaningful and beautiful life with God and others. When you nurture your soul, your life in this world will come to make sense again; you can find your way back to God from hope-lessness, depression, relationship struggles, and a lack of fulfill-ment. Your soul's resting place is in God, and John Ortberg wants to take participants to that home.

This study guide with DVD includes a DVD with six video teaching sessions from John Ortberg and a study guide with discussion questions, video notes, and in-between studies.

Sessions include:

1. What Is the Soul?
2. The Struggle of the Soul
3. What the Soul Needs
4. The Practice of Grace
5. The Practice of Gratitude
6. The Practice of Growth

Available in stores and online!

ZONDERVAN®
.com

Who Is This Man?

Bestselling Author John Ortberg

Jesus's impact on our world is highly unlikely, widely inescapable, largely unknown, and decidedly double-edged. It is unlikely in light of the severe limitations of his earthly life; it is inescapable because of the range of impact; it is unknown because history doesn't connect dots; and it is doubled-edged because his followers have wreaked so much havoc, often in his name. He is history's most familiar figure, yet he is the man no one knows. His impact on the world is immense and non-accidental. From the Dark Ages to Post-Modernity he is the Man who won't go away. And yet ... you can miss him in historical lists for many reasons, maybe the most obvious being the way he lived his life. He did not loudly and demonstrably defend his movement in the spirit of a rising political or military leader. He did not lay out a case that history would judge his brand of belief superior in all future books. His life and teaching simply drew people to follow him. He made history by starting in a humble place, in a spirit of love and acceptance, and allowing each person space to respond. His vision of life continues to haunt and challenge humanity. His influence has swept over history bringing inspiration to what has happened in art, science, government, medicine, and education; he has taught humans about dignity, compassion, forgiveness, and hope.

Who Is This Man? DVD

Bestselling Author John Ortberg

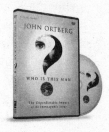

In this five-session DVD-based small group bible study, *Who Is This Man?* John Ortberg reveals how Jesus made an inescapable influence on our world and you will learn how you can make one too.

Sessions include:

1. *The Man Who Won't Go Away*

2. *A Revolution of Humanity*

3. *The Power of Forgiveness*

4. *Why It's a Small World After All*

5. *Three Days That Changed the World*

The Life You've Always Wanted

Spiritual Disciples for Ordinary People

John Ortberg

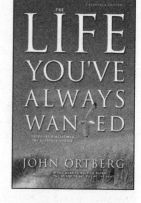

What does true spiritual life really look like? What keeps you from living such a life? What can you do to pursue it? If you're tired of the status quo—if you suspect that there is more to Christianity than what you've experienced—John Ortberg points to a road of transformation and spiritual vigor that anyone can take. It is the road that leads to *The Life You've Always Wanted*.

The Christian life is about more than being forgiven, more even than making it to heaven. John Ortberg calls us back to the dynamic heart of Christianity—God's power to bring change and growth—and shows us how we can attain it …and why we should attain it. *The Life You've Always Wanted* offers modern perspectives on the ancient path of the spiritual disciplines. Ortberg shows us that Christianity isn't a matter of externals, of outer form that gets the church stamp of approval, but of Christ's character becoming etched with ever-increasing depth into our own character.

As with a marathon runner, the secret lies not in trying harder, but in training consistently. Hence the spiritual disciplines. They're neither taskmasters nor an end in themselves. They're exercises that strengthen our endurance race down the road of growth. As we continue down that road, we'll see the signposts of joy, peace, and kindness, and all the hallmarks of a faith that's vital, real, and growing.

Paved with humor and sparkling anecdotes, *The Life You've Always Wanted* is an encouraging and challenging approach to a Christian life that's worth living. Life on the edge that fills our ordinary world with new meaning, hope, change, and a joyous, growing closeness to Christ.

When the Game Is Over, It All Goes Back in the Box

John Ortberg

Remember the thrill of winning at checkers or Parcheesi? You become the Master of the Board — the victor over everyone else. But what happens after that? asks bestselling author John Ortberg. You know the answer: It all goes back in the box. You don't get to keep one token, one chip, one game card. In the end, the spoils of the game add up to nothing.

Using popular games as a metaphor for our temporal lives, *When the Game Is Over, It All Goes Back in the Box* neatly sorts out what's fleeting and what's permanent in God's kingdom. Being Master of the Board is not the point; being rich toward God is. Winning the game of life on Earth is a temporary victory; loving God and other people with all our hearts is an eternal one. Using humor, terrific stories, and a focus on winning "the right trophies," Ortberg paints a vivid picture of the priorities that all Christians will want to embrace.

When the Game Is Over, It All Goes Back in the Box
Six Sessions on Living Life in the Light of Eternity

John Ortberg with Stephen and Amanda Sorenson

In the six sessions you will learn how to:
- Live passionately and boldly
- Learn how to be active players in the game that pleases God
- Find your true mission and offer your best
- Fill each square on the board with what matters most
- Seek the richness of being instead of the richness of having

Everybody's Normal Till You Get to Know Them

John Ortberg

Not you, that's for sure! No one you've ever met, either. None of us are normal according to God's definition, and the closer we get to each other, the plainer that becomes.

Yet for all our quirks, sins, and jagged edges, we need each other. Community is more than just a word — it is one of our most fundamental requirements. So how do flawed, abnormal people such as ourselves master the forces that can drive us apart and come together in the life-changing relationships God designed us for?

In *Everybody's Normal Till You Get to Know Them*, teacher and bestselling author John Ortberg zooms in on the things that make community tick. You'll get a thought-provoking look at God's heart, at others, and at yourself. Even better, you'll gain wisdom and tools for drawing closer to others in powerful, impactful ways. With humor, insight, and a gift for storytelling, Ortberg shows how community pays tremendous dividends in happiness, health, support, and growth. It's where all of us weird, unwieldy people encounter God's love in tangible ways and discover the transforming power of being loved, accepted, and valued just the way we are.

Available in stores and online!

God Is Closer Than You Think

This Can Be the Greatest Moment of Your Life Because This Moment Is the Place Where You Can Meet God

John Ortberg

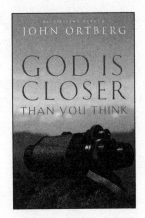

Intimacy with God can happen right now if you want it. A closeness you can feel, a goodness you can taste, a reality you can experience for yourself. That's what the Bible promises, so why settle for less? God is closer than you think, and connecting with him isn't for monks and ascetics. It's for business people, high school students, busy moms, single men, single women … and most important, it's for YOU.

God Is Closer Than You Think shows how you can enjoy a vibrant, moment-by-moment relationship with your heavenly Father. Bestselling author John Ortberg reveals the face of God waiting to be discovered in the complex mosaic of your life. He shows you God's hand stretching toward you. And, with his gift for storytelling, Ortberg illustrates the ways you can reach toward God and complete the connection—to your joy and his.

Available in stores and online!

ZONDERVAN®
.com

God Is Closer
Than You Think

ZondervanGroupware™
Small Group Edition

John Ortberg with
Stephen & Amanda Sorenson

The story of the Bible is the story of God's desire to be with his people. God is extending himself, stretching out to reach us and to fill our lives with his presence. Every moment of your life is like a page in a Where's Waldo book. God is there, the Scriptures tell us, but the ease with which he may be found varies from one page to the next. God is closer than you think!

The curriculum kit provides sermon resources and promotional materials for the pastor, small group materials for discussion in groups, and a sample copy of the hardcover book that everyone can read on their own. The kit includes a six-session small group participant's guide, a six-session DVD featuring John Ortberg, a thirty-two-page leader's guide, a CD-ROM with sermon resources and promotional materials, and one copy of the hardcover book.

Available in stores and online!

ZONDERVAN®
.com

Old Testament Challenge

Help your congregation experience the life-changing relevance of the Old Testament

The Old Testament Challenge (OTC) is a turnkey program to help everyone in your church understand and apply the Old Testament. Participants experience the content in multiple contexts: through sermons, group discussions, and personal devotions.

This 32-week series is designed for churches to teach, study, and discuss the entire Old Testament over a 9-month period. The goal of OTC is to discover the life-changing truths of the Old Testament and how they can be applied to daily life. Based on Pastor John Ortberg's OTC series at the New Community services of Willow Creek Community Church, this resource enables churches to raise the level of biblical literacy and understanding among their congregations. Your congregation will fall in love with the Old Testament!

The OTC curriculum is made up of 4 kits of 7–9 lessons each. This first kit covers the Pentateuch and includes everything you need to preach 9 sermons (that's less than $25 per week!):

- Teaching Guide containing material from Ortberg's weekly teachings for pastors and/or teachers

- Group Discussion Guide focusing on specific passages from the Old Testament designed for weekly or bi-weekly use and including leader's notes
- DVD and VHS Video presenting an OTC "vision-casting" message from Ortberg, a promotional piece for churches, and 4 creative video elements for each kit to use during the OTC message
- CD-ROM providing 7-9 PowerPoint® presentations for use with each of the OTC messages. It also contains 40 FAQ sheets answering tough questions from the Old Testament for use on your website or to be printed in hard copy.
- Sets of slides for each teaching session for pastors and teachers.
- Sermon Audio CD set containing all 9 messages preached by John Ortberg
- Implementation Guide
- 40 Weeks with God reading guide

Old Testament Challenge---Kit 1: 978-0-310-24891-4
Old Testament Challenge---Kit 2: 978-0-310-24931-7
Old Testament Challenge---Kit 3: 978-0-310-25031-5
Old Testament Challenge---Kit 4: 978-0-310-25142-7

Available in stores and online!

WILLOW CREEK ASSOCIATION

This resource is just one of many ministry tools published in partnership with the Willow Creek Association. Founded in 1992, WCA was created to serve churches and church leaders striving to create environments where those still outside the family of God are welcomed—and can more easily consider God's loving offer of salvation through faith.

These innovative churches and leaders are connected at the deepest level by their all-out dedication to Christ and His Kingdom. Willing to do whatever it required to build churches that help people move along the path toward Christ-centered devotion; they also share a deep desire to encourage all believers at every step of their faith journey, to continue moving toward a fully transformed, Christ-centered life.

Today, more than 10,000 churches from 80 denominations worldwide are formally connected to WCA and each other through WCA Membership. Many thousands more come to WCA for networking, training, and resources.

For more information about the ministry of the
Willow Creek Association, visit: **willowcreek.com**.